"*Total Parish Development* is a m
desire to nurture a dynamic pari
ty-first century. Frank Donaldsor
clues for preparing parishes to seize the moment and courageously
advance forward. This is one of the best practical resources!"

■ SISTER ANGELA ANN ZUKOWSKI, MHSH, DMIN, THE INSTITUTE FOR
PASTORAL INITIATIVES, PROFESSOR, DEPARTMENT OF RELIGIOUS STUDIES,
UNIVERSITY OF DAYTON

"Here at St. Ann, we have put ISPD's processes into place and have
seen a transformation that has turned us into a thriving parish.
Whether you are a growing parish or a parish in decline, the information in this book and Frank's experience in development will take
you to a level you would never imagine."

■ TIM CLIFFORD, DIRECTOR OF STEWARDSHIP & DEVELOPMENT,
ST. ANN PARISH, ARCHDIOCESE OF CINCINNATI, OHIO

"In *Total Parish Development*, Frank provides a step-by-step, eye-
ball-to-eyeball process to inspire others to be engaged in a meaningful, Spirit-filled ministry to do something great with their lives that
will reinvent their parish. This engagement of others will refresh and
revitalize the parish's efforts to build God's kingdom."

■ REGINA HANEY, EDD, EXECUTIVE DIRECTOR, NATIONAL ASSOCIATION OF
CHURCH PERSONNEL ADMINISTRATORS (NACPA)

"*Total Parish Development* is a patient process, but like the parable of
the mustard seed in the gospel, it bears much fruit. When people
believe that they are 'called,' they tend to give more of themselves. This
is all about people, not money. Money is a by-product of involvement
and engagement."

■ FATHER JAMES MANNING, PASTOR, ST. MARY OF THE ASSUMPTION PARISH,
ARCHDIOCESE OF CINCINNATI

"Great foundation. Great principles. Thorough and thought-provoking information for anyone working in parish leadership in the twenty-first century!"

■ FATHER JAMES COMMYN, PASTOR, ST. LUCY PARISH, ARCHDIOCESE OF DETROIT

"*Total Parish Development* provides helpful tools for the implementation of a total process of growth and development. I highly recommend it to pastors, parochial administrators, principals, and parish leaders."

■ FATHER CHRISTIAN TABARES, VICAR FOR SPANISH MINISTRY, PASTOR
OF ST. ELIZABETH OF HUNGARY PARISH AND ST. FRANCES XAVIER CABRINI
PARISH, DIOCESE OF SAGINAW

"Our parish seeks to become a band of joyful missionary disciples. Thanks to Frank's counsel and development process, we are pointed in the right direction and making great strides to that end. We benefited greatly from his guidance and his process."

■ JUAN BALBOA, FORMER PARISH COUNCIL PRESIDENT; NATIONAL SHRINE OF
THE LITTLE FLOWER BASILICA; ARCHDIOCESE OF DETROIT

"In early 2018, we realized we needed to raise parish engagement and start a development ministry. Several members took Frank's *Total Parish Development* online courses through the University of Dayton. We learned not only the basics of people engagement and development, but we also learned effective methods to establish an entire development ministry. We are now successfully up and running."

■ BILL RECTANUS, CHAIRMAN, AND KEVIN STOGRAN, VICE-CHAIRMAN, OF THE
PARISH COUNCIL, ST. ELIZABETH PARISH, DIOCESE OF COLUMBUS, OHIO

"At St. Ladislas Parish, we have put into action on a daily basis the expression 'belonging leads to believing.' The true measure of our success has been sustainability. We started this process with ISPD in 2012 and it is now a way of life in our parish."

■ BUD TETZLAFF, PARISH LEADER, ST. LADISLAS PARISH,
DIOCESE OF COLUMBUS, OHIO

TOTAL PARISH DEVELOPMENT

UNDERSTANDING, ORGANIZING
and **IMPLEMENTING** *Your Plan for*
an Engaged Catholic Community

FRANK DONALDSON

TWENTY-THIRD PUBLICATIONS
twentythirdpublications.com

Twenty-Third Publications
One Montauk Avenue, Suite 200
New London, CT 06320
(860) 437-3012 or (800) 321-0411
www.twentythirdpublications.com

Images:
Cover: iStock.com / HenryPhotos
page 11: iStock.com / BlackJack3D

ISBN: 978-1-62785-483-2
Printed in the U.S.A.

A division of Bayard, Inc.

CONTENTS

ACKNOWLEDGMENTS

Thank you to all the Catholic leaders with whom we have worked and are working who have provided and continue to provide the inspiration to move beyond mediocrity and build stronger communities of faith that bring us all closer to Christ.

Thank you to Sister Mary Ann Hardcastle, RSM, for giving me the opportunity to begin this ministry. Your encouragement and belief in the beginning years have never been forgotten.

Thank you to Father Jim Manning and Father Dennis Hartigan, two priests who have helped nurture and promote the mission and vision of ISPD for many years. Thank you for your friendship, your ministry, and your affirmation that Catholic Development is all about engaging people in order to help build the Kingdom of God.

Thank you to Father Frank Lipps (1942 – 2016) and Father Kyle Dave, the wonderful pastors who served at Our Lady of Lourdes in Slidell, LA and who were instrumental in bringing the parish together in the aftermath of Hurricane Katrina in 2005. Thank you for your leadership, your understanding, and your ability to engage and connect with people.

Thank you to Father Tom Ranzino in the Diocese of Baton Rouge who has always stood as such a meaningful model to my family of what a pastor should be—kind, engaging, interested, understanding, knowledgeable, and faith-filled.

Thank you to ISPD's National Board of Advisors for continuing to provide direction, encouragement, and belief.

Thank you to Sister Angela Ann Zukowski, Director, The Institute for Pastoral Initiatives at The University of Dayton for forming the partnership we have in teaching Catholic Parish Development leaders throughout the country.

Thank you to the hundreds of students in our on-line classes (representing over 100 dioceses) for being the motivators and inspiration for *Total Parish Development.*

Thank you to the dedicated staff and associates of ISPD, who believe in the mission and the vision and continue the journey—Tony Bonura, Joe Therber, Dr. Erik Goldschmidt, Ken Barlag, Dr. Regina Haney, Karen Hintz, and Ryan Zellner.

Thank you to my wife, Suzy, for your understanding of the many nights away from home and the crazy schedule I keep—you are the main motivation and inspiration that keep this vision alive.

Thank you to my daughter Megan, who as a college senior, continues to grow in her faith as a Catholic. You continue to make us proud as you navigate the challenging road of life and recognize your relationship with Christ should be at the center of all you do.

Lastly, thank you to my three adult daughters, Lisa, Shannon and Cheri. You all have overcome difficult challenges; you have grown, matured, and lead meaningful lives with your faith strong and steadfast.

FOREWORD

> "Do not be afraid. Do not be satisfied with mediocrity. Put out into the deep and let down your nets for a catch." SAINT JOHN PAUL II

In order to be successful in anything we do, we have to have passion and a desire to be the very best that we can be. I often refer to that as "fire in the belly." By that, I do not mean being "top dog" or the "star" or the "hot shot." I simply mean, taking the gifts that God has given us, developing those gifts, continuously working to improve them, and then making them work for the good of our cause(s). In our work across the country at the Institute for School and Parish Development (ISPD), we see many Catholic leaders who possess that "fire in the belly."

As parish leaders, we all have similar missions: to develop and advance our parishes by engaging people to help us build the kingdom of God. This is an awesome responsibility. As many of us know, this work is not for the weak of heart; it is not for those who quit early; and it is not for those who want to raise a "quick buck" or "hit somebody up for money." Being part of a vibrant Catholic parish development effort is rewarding, enriching, and fulfilling. Done properly, for the right reasons, this ministry helps us to develop and grow as stewards. It puts order into our lives, as we realize that our lives are not just about us; they are about doing God's work and what God wants to *develop*. Properly understood, our ministry calls us to reach out as Jesus did and, despite the naysayers and those who only want to guard their kingdom, bring people

1

closer to him. In our Catholic parishes, we can have an impact on so many lives—from the new family who arrives with eager anticipation at their first Mass, to the person we see only at Easter, to the family who is going through challenging times.

But where do we develop this passion? How do we come to realize that this work of Catholic parish development is so much more than running a fund-raiser or "tapping" someone for money? How do we get away from always measuring what we do by the question, "How much money did you raise?" True Catholic parish development is much deeper.

My own journey into true Catholic parish development started with a family tragedy. In 1986, I lost my five-year-old son, Dustin. He died of an illness (rhabdomyolysis) that impacts few children. One day he was here, and then four days later he was not. What adds deeper meaning to his passing is that he started complaining about his legs cramping on Good Friday, and then he passed away on Easter Monday afternoon. Every Lent, our family's faith becomes magnified through the remembrance of his death.

Dustin was a very likable child—always smiling, always laughing, always having a cheery twinkle in his eye. He attended St. Rosalie Catholic School in Harvey, Louisiana, and was a favorite of many of his teachers and the principal, Sister Jeanne. He was elected king of the Mardi Gras at the school and loved every minute of the attention. He was hardly ever down or sad, and even when he was punished for doing something crazy, it was only a matter of minutes before he would bounce back. One day he came home from school and announced that he was going to be a priest! Five years old and a priest?

Although Dustin always had a smile and a kind word, he frequently battled with illnesses, and so during Holy Week it really wasn't a huge surprise when he complained about cramping in his legs. On Friday, his mother took him to the doctor and then on Saturday he was in the hospital—supposedly just for precaution. By Monday morning, things had turned for the worst as he was rushed to the operating room with a heart attack, and it was then that we realized he might be in his last hours.

I will never forget the doctor at Ochsner Hospital coming to us and, in tears, saying, "We have done all that we can do. He will not live much longer, so please, go now and say your good-byes."

It's funny how moments like that are branded in your mind. I remember walking into the OR and looking at my son as he lay on an operating table. He was in pain, but he still had that smile. As I tried to maintain my composure, he looked up and the last words he said to me were, "Daddy, I'm going to be with Jesus."

Dustin passed away Easter Monday afternoon at 3:42.

The next year was a blur. I was offered a job teaching English at Mercy Academy in New Orleans during that 1986–1987 school year. Sister Mary Ann Hardcastle, RSM, hired me. I really don't know how I made it through that year; the pain was great and getting up every morning was a chore. All of us who have lost loved ones know the feelings and the struggles, and yet there is a faint desire to overcome and build something that will take us to the next day. Two thoughts kept running through my mind that year. I had a sociology teacher in college, Dr. Ben Kaplan, who reminded us how much better it was "to light a candle rather than curse the darkness." I remembered that, and I also remembered my son's last words. Those were the two threads that I hung on to—one of hope and one of faith.

Time moved on and the healing began. Life may shut a lot of doors, but God always gives us a window somewhere; we just need to find it. Gradually the pain moved into energy, and I developed a strong desire to do something meaningful—something that would make a difference. I moved into administration, then into development at Mercy Academy, and then, in 1989, there was a voice inside of me calling out to begin a new ministry. And so, with a leap of real faith, I left the security of a regular Catholic school paycheck and started the Institute for School and Parish Development. I have never looked back.

The fire that burned so strongly years ago is still alive and still as powerful as ever. So many times, as I leave home and head out on the road for another week in another city, I ask myself, "Why am I doing this?" And the answer comes back immediately: "You do it because of Dustin and because you have gifts to share and a family that believes in and supports you." There was a reason my son was able to say what he said, and I owe it to the faith community of St. Rosalie Parish and School. They were very instrumental in developing Dustin's faith—so much so that he even considered being a priest, and so much so that his final words echoed his belief in his maker. He did not get to that point alone; a pastor, a principal, and many others were greatly responsible for bringing him to that point in his life. And I cannot help but believe that Christ was there to hold his hand as he crossed to the other side.

The death of my son was the birth of this ministry. In my anguish, God gave me a lifeline and hope for the future. I have been blessed countless times since 1986—with my wife Suzy and my daughter Megan, and my older daughters, Lisa, Shannon, and Cheri, and nine grandchildren. In fact, my oldest grandson, Jordan, was born the day after Dustin's birthday: September 26. God works in wonderful ways.

Years ago, we started the Dustin Ewing Donaldson Memorial Scholarship at St. Rosalie, where at graduation a member of our family has the opportunity to award an outstanding graduate who is going to continue his/her education in a Catholic high school with scholarship money for their first year. The faculty and staff vote for the recipient based on the traits we always attributed to Dustin:

- Courage,
- Pleasing, smiling personality,
- Always reaching out to help others,
- Unconditional love,
- Belief in the love of Jesus Christ,
- Polite and well-mannered.

A plaque with Dustin's picture and the names of the recipients for each year hangs in the lobby of St. Rosalie Catholic School in Harvey, Louisiana.

"Fire in the belly." It pushes us onward and brings about introspection, motivation, and purpose. My journey is not unique, for there are thousands just like me. However, my quest has always been the same—to work with a diocese or a parish or a Catholic school and, through the gifts God has given me, to really make a difference in helping build a stronger faith community, to help bring that Catholic institution *to total parish development*. And possibly, even in the smallest degree—through this ministry—to help bring others, and myself, closer to Christ, so that we all, in our final hour might be able to say, "Daddy, I'm going to be with Jesus."

PART I

Introduction

History and Rationale

In 2015, I wrote a book titled *25 Lessons Learned in 25+ Years in Catholic School Development*. It was published by the National Catholic Educational Association (NCEA) in March 2016. Shortly thereafter, I wrote a workbook to accompany the text, published by NCEA in November 2017, and the Institute for School and Parish Development now use both publications to teach Catholic schools about setting up successful development and advancement efforts.

At the time, I did not realize the need for such publications, but this became very noticeable when ISPD—Institute for School and Parish Development, the Catholic consulting company I founded in 1989—formed a partnership with the University of Dayton in 2017, and we, along with Sister Angela Zukowski, MHSH, D.Min., executive director for the Institute for Pastoral Initiatives, began to teach online certificate courses using the textbook and the workbook. The first ten-lesson course was offered in the fall of 2017, and we had 190 students enrolled from across the country. As of the spring semester 2019, we now have taught over 1,000 students (superintendents, principals, pastors, presidents, development and/or advancement officers, board members, faculty/staff, parent volunteers, etc.). People from more than 100 dioceses have participated in *25 Lessons Learned: Part I* and *Part II*.

It is through these relationships, connections, and associations that we realized the unbelievable *thirst* that leaders in Catholic institutions have for learning more about development. Many do not have the time or the budget to attend faraway conferences and conventions, but they are able to learn with an online course where they can receive Continuing Education Units (CEUs) and a Certificate of Completion from The University of Dayton.

Therefore, after we completed the textbook and workbook in Catholic school development, many people encouraged us to do the same for Catholic parishes—where the need is just as great, if not greater. We now are excited to offer a combination textbook/workbook in Catholic Parish Development—made possible by having worked as a Catholic parish/school consultant for the past 30+ years throughout the country.

In addition, in the fall of 2018, we added a course to the curriculum we are offering through the University of Dayton—*Catholic Parish Development: Beyond Mediocrity*. This course, which we are now teaching, has 112 students from 52 dioceses. We are following the fifteen lessons of this book, *Total Parish Development*, and the response and the discussions and sharing of homework assignments has been contagious. Many parishes are excited about learning, and a number of parishes, not being content with doing what they have always done, are "putting out their nets into the deep." They seem to be ready for real cultural change. As one student recently stated in his final exam project, "The real challenge for our parish leaders was actually understanding the real meaning of *Catholic Parish Development*."

I would like to share these experiences and lessons with you. I only wish I would have had someone or something to guide me along the way and let me know what to do and what not to do when I was starting my development journey. There is a lot that is available in development/advancement for Catholic schools, but there is not a lot that is available in development for Catholic parishes. Sure, there are fund-raising companies and webinars on how to write letters and how to increase your offertory giving. There are companies that can come in and show you how to run a capital campaign. There are database companies, special event companies, and others. But that is not what this book is about. This publication and this journey are about teaching you how to set up and establish a successful Catholic Parish Development *system* in your parish—one that will invite and involve people, and one that will move your parish to *total* parish development. If ever in the history of the Catholic Church there were a time when we needed to reach out and affirm, welcome, and engage, now is that time.

PART II

Philosophy and Fundamentals of Catholic Parish Development

> "Our Christian identity is belonging to a people: the Church. Without the Church we are not Christians."
> POPE FRANCIS

Lesson One: Understand Catholic Parish Development and Its Importance

The first two decades of the twenty-first century might long be remembered as challenging years in this country, and, more specifically, in the Catholic Church. The events of September 11th, the constant ups and downs of the economy, the closing of a number of Catholic churches and schools, and daily headlines addressing the sexual misconduct of some clergy—these have all rocked the foundation of many Catholic dioceses, parishes, and schools. Those of us who work in the ministry of developing Catholic institutions continue to be challenged and to be called upon to set forth positive action that will build community, engage people, and build faith in our Catholic parishes and schools. The call for leadership has never been stronger. In fact, just today, I received an e-mail from one of my students in the online class I am teaching in Catholic school development who said, "The Catholic 'pull' is

9

not very popular this year. I am in a highly rated public-school district, so competition is tough. Timing is bad with the child abuse priest scandal that just came out across our state. I don't want to downplay a faith-centered school, but it is not a 'pull' right now. Any suggestions?"

CATHOLIC DEVELOPMENT: A KEY ANSWER

There are several ways to address these challenges, but the one that we see making the most impact is *development*. A key word. A key initiative. Unfortunately, it is a word that has been misunderstood for many years. So many Catholic leaders see development as the main way of getting money for their parish and/or school. Whereas fund-raising can be one of the components of development, as we stated in the Introduction, we see development in a broader sense. We define development as *the meaningful involvement of people in your mission and vision for the future*. And the key word is *meaningful*. People do want to get involved; people do want to feel like they belong.

With all that has happened, there continues to be a strong cry throughout this country for Catholic institutions to straighten their ship, create a dynamic vision and plan, chart a course of positive direction, invite hundreds to get involved, and then set sail. In the past at many parishes and schools, this has been done with a selected circle of people; today, we find that more and more folks want to be invited; they want to belong; they want to help create that new vision, that new plan, that new ministry, that new program.

It is all about engaging people. By analogy, here is what we see over and over every day in this ministry of Catholic consulting. In most parishes and schools, if I drop a pebble in a pond, the first ripple is usually about 25–50 people. These are usually the leaders, the ones who are asked to do everything. They are the parish council members, the festival chairs, the ministry leaders, and those on the finance committee. And, if the truth be known, most parishes and schools could not do without them. The problem? Possible burnout, and many times these people are always asked to do everything; therefore, very few new people become involved. It usually points to a statement that we at ISPD strongly believe: *The greatest challenge we face today in our Catholic parishes and schools is not raising money. The greatest challenge we face is in creating the roadways, avenues, and vehicles to invite, involve, and engage people.*

The second ripple is another 50 or more people who do not get involved, and they do not step forward because of one basic reason: no one invites them—*personally*. We create bulletin and newsletter announcements, put out flyers, post on our website, ask people to sign up for this and that, send out social media messages and e-mails, but very few Catholic leaders actually extend a personal invitation—eyeball to eyeball. There is one thing that years and years of consulting has taught us here at ISPD:

- When a person is invited to become involved by means of "paper" (letter, e-mail, bulletin, flyer, website, social media post, newsletter, etc.), 5%–8% respond positively;
- When a person is invited over the telephone, 15%–18% respond positively;
- When a person is invited to become involved, and the invitation is "eyeball to eyeball" and dialogue is present, then 45%–55% respond positively.

In addition, there are also third and fourth ripples from that pebble, and these are people who are not even known. They are neighbors, uninvolved parishioners, friends of the parish, vendors, community members, and more. What we have seen is that most Catholic parish leaders know 20%–30% of their parishioner base and no more. These leaders may know names, addresses, phone numbers, and e-mails, and have the ability to say "Hi" and "Hello." But as far as actually knowing the people, their talents, their gifts, and their resources? Most Catholic institutions simply do not have the processes set up and the personnel in place to identify, invite, and involve. Just think of the hundreds and hundreds of "people resources" every parish has right at their fingertips. The key is setting up the development efforts to invite and involve these folks in a meaningful manner. Once people become involved, they then begin to take ownership, and a partnership develops. Once that sense of investment is present, the sky is the limit. Yet it all goes back to people, to personal invitations, to relationships, and to seeing development as the means of achieving that end. And what a wonderful time to invite and involve people in a meaningful manner. Development is the key. But we must be willing to change; we must shift the paradigm. We must formalize Catholic Parish Development.

ENGAGEMENT OF PEOPLE: THE LATEST DATA

If we agree that development is the ministry that helps the People of God find the structures for involvement and engagement, then it is also important that we understand the importance of engaging people. What is engagement? According to the Gallup Organization, think of it as the transmission in your car. When it is engaged, the gears mesh and the car moves. But if it is in neutral, the gears spin, but you do not get anywhere. It is like that in many parishes. Many people are very active, appearing to be doing a lot of important work. But activity can happen without any progress being made. The gears aren't meshing; they are not engaged. And without engagement, the parish cannot move forward in accomplishing its mission.

Webster's International Dictionary says this about the word engagement: "Act of being involved, greatly interested. A favorable attachment."

In interviewing thousands of people over a period of years, the Gallup Organization has made some dynamic discoveries. In debunking some old myths, they have discovered a new set of paradigms that are fast replacing conventional leadership wisdom. Here are three of them:

1. **Myth:** Believing leads to belonging.
   - According to Gallup analysis, this myth has been turned upside down. In reality, belonging is far more likely to lead to believing. The extent to which a member feels engaged in a community has a profound impact on his/her personal spiritual commitment.

2. **Myth:** An active member is a faithful member.
   - Gallup research has discovered that activity that is not the result of engagement leads to burnout. And burned-out members eventually leave. In religious institutions where there is activity without engagement, terms such as "duty" and "responsibility" are repeated in recruiting volunteers for roles. And often the response to such recruiting is, "I've done my share. It's time for the younger members to take their turn."
   - In contrast, engaged members are those who regularly have the opportunity to do what they do best, because the leadership of that parish has invested the time needed to discover each member's talents and strengths.
   - Engaged members do not burn out; they only become stronger, more energized, and more engaged.

3. **Myth:** Personal faith leads to public action.
   - Outcomes such as how much a member gives financially, how many hours she/he volunteers in service to the parish, and how often she/he invites others to become part of that faith community are more dependent on his/her level of engagement than any other factor.

In ISPD's definition of development, the key word we have emphasized is *meaningful*. Development is the *meaningful* involvement of people in your mission and your vision for the future. *Meaningful* distinguishes between the volunteer at the bingo hall selling pull tabs and the technology guru who, as a new parishioner, gives the gift of setting up an interactive website for the parish. *Meaningful* distinguishes between the volunteers who haul a case of two-liter Pepsi to the parish center for the Friday Night Fish Fry and the parishioner who, as a horticulturist, decides to plant and grow a beautiful rose garden along the barren walkway outside of church. *Meaningful* distinguishes between the parishioner who volunteers for four hours at the plant booth at the fair and the parishioner who, as a master carpenter by profession, is in charge of designing and building the forty-two booths at the parish festival. Engagement is indeed a favorable attachment.

All of the above tasks are important in Catholic parishes; however, when a task is matched with a person's interests, gifts, and skills, then we find that the person becomes more engaged and feels a stronger sense of ownership.

To make this all come alive, in 1989, ISPD created our 7-"I" process. Through the years we have taught, written, and implemented these 7 "I" words in everything we do as Catholic development consultants. These 7 "I"s are the "plays" that make the game come alive. They force us to emphasize the people, the process, and the ministry of Catholic development. The 7-"I" process is the major vehicle for engaging people. Let us review.

THE 7 "I"S OF CATHOLIC PARISH DEVELOPMENT

Identify: Continually identify the people who will and can make a difference in your parish.

Inform: Using all of the tools in the communication toolbox, reach out to all members of the parish community, informing them how your parish is developing and advancing.

Invite: Personally invite people to belong—eyeball to eyeball.

Involve: Involve people in development processes in meaningful ways.

Implement: Put into action strategic plans and initiatives that have been created through people involvement.

Invest: Arrange for involved people to invest in the future of their parish and their own personal spiritual growth.

Improve: Implement an evaluative process to ensure longevity of the development process.

We invite you to view the 7 "I"s as one big circle that is constantly spinning, and inside of that circle are 7 smaller circles that are also constantly spinning. This energy—built around engaging people—creates the development efforts that will bring positive results.

MOVING FORWARD

As parishes continue to wrap their heads around this word *development*, most are faced with challenges that need to be successfully solved.

- How can we continue to build trust in our Catholic leaders?
- How can we evangelize more people in the midst of change?
- How can we communicate better?
- How can we engage more people to make a difference?
- How can we reach the young people of our parish?
- How can we address and integrate the growing Hispanic communities in our parish?
- How can we identify and encourage those who could be called to religious vocation and priestly leadership?
- How can we make sure that Jesus is the heart of all that we do?
- How can we make sure that all parishes understand the real meaning of Catholic Parish Development and move forward in implementation?

These are daunting challenges. Yet there are answers contained in the lessons in this book, answers that point the way to a bright future. Not THE answer, but answers; however, we must be willing to change. It all begins with people; it continues with the creation or the re-creation of the mission and the vision. Assessment is the next step, which leads to planning and implementation. Along the journey, more people are engaged; processes are initiated, and the ministry of Catholic Parish Development begins or continues to flourish. It may be a mystery to some, but to those who understand the true meaning of development, the importance of engagement, and the 7 "I"s in motion, there has never been a better time for this ministry to flourish. Development can come more alive than ever in our parishes. Our journey is not undertaken alone:

- The Father encourages us,
- The Son directs us,
- The Spirit anoints us.

Our challenge, today and beyond, is to seize the moment, move to total parish development, and journey with Christ to help build the kingdom.

Questions, Exercises, and Next Best Steps for Lesson One

1. How do your parish leaders define the word "development"?

2. With the definition of "Catholic Parish Development" being used in Lesson One (the meaningful involvement of people), what individuals/groups in your parish understand this definition? Please check all that apply.

☐ Pastor   ☐ Parish staff
☐ Parish council   ☐ Finance council
☐ Stewardship ministry   ☐ Other: _____

3. What processes do you have in place to make sure that you are identifying and personally getting to know all new families who move into the parish?

4. When seeking to invite people to various events, activities, ministries, leadership positions, etc., what percentage of the invitations are done personally, with phone calls and "eyeball to eyeball" invitations? Please explain.

5. For those people who do raise their hands to help, are you set up and organized to personally follow up and engage them in the life of the parish? Please explain.

6. As you look at the families in your parish and their involvement level, what percentages would you apply to the following:

   _____ Involved/Engaged (involved in ministries, attends Mass on regular/consistent basis, financially participates on weekly basis)

   _____ Uninvolved (not involved in any ministry, attends Mass once a month, and does not financially participate at all)

   _____ Actively Disengaged (only see them on Christmas, Easter, and when daughter needs to be married, child needs to be baptized, and/or spouse needs to be buried)

7. Using the 7-"I" approach that is explained in this lesson, please fill in the following information.

   IDENTIFY A Please check all of the different individual and groups of parishioners and non-parishioners who are, or could be, important to the mission/vision of your parish—where you have accurate contact information.

   ☐ Names of parish council members

- ☐ Names of finance council members

- ☐ Names of ministry leaders for each ministry

- ☐ Names of ministry members in each ministry

- ☐ Names of parish staff members

- ☐ Names of school administration, faculty/staff, and parents (if applicable)

- ☐ Names of parishioners not in the above groups

- ☐ Names of vendors

- ☐ Names of key civic community leaders

- ☐ Names of key diocesan leaders

- ☐ Names of key financial leaders (people who give more than $1,000/year)

IDENTIFY B In addition, with your parishioners, explain how you identify their interests, skills, talents, and gifts.

INFORM Please list all of the ways you communicate with the people you listed above.

INVITE With all of the events, activities, ministries, and happenings in your parish, please list those where people are personally—by phone or in person—invited to attend and/or belong.

INVOLVE Please list all of the events, activities, and ministries in your parish that involve and target the newest parishioners year to year.

IMPLEMENT Please list all of the processes, ministries, and activities where the people you personally involve actually help you implement.

INVEST Please list any activities, events, ministries, and processes where you believe people in your parish really become involved in a meaningful way and actually see themselves as true stewards of the parish—as a result of that involvement.

IMPROVE Because of the theme of continuous improvement, please describe the ways that you and those around you seek to professionally develop and get better from year to year. In addition, please describe what process(es) you use to assess and improve all of the ministries in your parish on an annual basis.

Lesson Two: Clarify the Differences: Development, Stewardship, and Evangelization

> "Evangelization does not consist in proselytizing, for proselytizing is a caricature of evangelization, but rather evangelizing entails attracting by our witness those who are far off, it means humbly drawing near to those who feel distant from God in the Church, drawing near to those who feel judged and condemned outright by those who consider themselves to be perfect and pure." POPE FRANCIS

In our work with Catholic parishes, it is important to understand what we mean by *Catholic Parish Development*. We find that three words need to be understood: *stewardship, development,* and *evangelization.* While it is true that these three words may be somewhat similar in meaning and function, for the sake of clarity, let us further distinguish.

Father Jim Manning, pastor of St. Mary of the Assumption Parish in Springboro, Ohio, and a long-time presenter at ISPD's workshops and seminars, has offered a wonderful explanation that should help define these words.

Stewardship is the biblical basis of development. It is the philosophy, the theology, and the spirituality behind development. In many of his parables, Jesus used the image of a "steward" to teach and remind his disciples that we are all accountable for the proper use and management of the gifts that have been entrusted to our care. Everything, including life itself, is a gift for which we need to be grateful. When all is said and done, stewardship is about gratitude. It reminds us that we all have the need to return thanks to God for the blessings that he has entrusted to us in life. Stewardship instills within us a "grateful heart."

Development is the ministry that puts a face on stewardship. The vision of the church articulated in the Second Vatican Council (*Lumen Gentium*) is that of the "people of God." Development is the ministry that can best incarnate this vision of church. As a ministry in the church, development provides the structures, the processes, and the avenues by which the People of God can do and live the spirituality of stewardship. Development helps the People of God live stewardship in an organized fashion. Development, as a ministry, positions the People of God on the same page and heading in the same direction as they live the gospel call to stewardship. Development helps the People of God live out their baptismal right and responsibility to be involved in the life of the church and thus share in the building of the kingdom of God here on earth. As we have said since the beginning days of our company: *Development is the meaningful involvement of people in your mission and vision for the future.* This enables and empowers the greatest amount of people to be involved in the life of the church (and the school). *Development helps accompany people in the journey of life back to the kingdom; it is the conduit for people engagement and true stewardship.* True Catholic development helps us "draw near" to people in all of the ripples in the pond.

In the process of fulfilling the call to stewardship in the ministry of development, *evangelization* is being done. Evangelization is preaching the Good News of Jesus.

Development brings the Good News of Jesus to the people of God in a structured, organized, and systemic way. As development helps the People of God find the structures for involvement and engagement in the life of the church and the ways and the means to live the gospel mission of stewardship, the Good News of Jesus is being taught, preached, and lived. Development as a ministry is actually developing and building the kingdom of God. When the ministry of development helps the people of God to give more of their time, wisdom, skills, prayers, connections, and resources, it actually is helping them develop a deeper relationship with the Lord. Giving our lives to the Lord as he did for us is the ultimate expression of stewardship and gratitude.

Questions, Exercises, and Next Best Steps for Lesson Two

1. How does your parish define the word "stewardship"?

2. Based on Lessons One and Two how would your parish leaders (clergy, parish council, parish staff, and finance council) differentiate between "development" and "stewardship"?

3. In your parish, do you have a team, committee, and/ or ministry that focuses on development? What about stewardship? Please explain.

4. What ways does your parish actively educate all parishioners on the meaning of true stewardship? Please explain.

5. In this age of the New Evangelization, what does your parish have in place to evangelize? Please explain.

Lesson Three: AWE: Understand the Importance of Affirming, Welcoming, and Engaging People in Your Catholic Parish

> "Have no fear of moving into the unknown. Simply step out fearlessly knowing that I am with you, therefore no harm can befall you; all is very, very well. Do this in complete faith and confidence."
>
> SAINT JOHN PAUL II

I had the wonderful opportunity in 2006 to present a two-day workshop at the priests' convocation in the Archdiocese of Baltimore. The title of the workshop was "Filling the Pews," and the subtitle was "Inviting, Welcoming, Engaging, and Affirming." Working with hundreds of priests for these two days was one of the highlights of my consulting career. They were interested, engaged, inquisitive, and eager to learn new ideas and processes, both from the presentation and from each other.

One of the by-products of that presentation was the chance to introduce this workshop to other dioceses throughout the country and actually work with individual parishes. One such diocese was the Diocese of Cleveland, where in 2012–2013 we offered a series of five workshops with over thirty parishes participating. Much of what we covered is integrated throughout this book; however, it was interesting to note that as the workshops unfolded, I could tell which parishes were going to take these ideas and lessons, adapt them to their own parish culture, and really surge forward. One such parish was St. Ladislas Parish in Westlake, Ohio. Bud Tetzlaff was one of the leaders in the parish, and after the last workshop Bud offered a wonderful suggestion: use the acronym AWE as the title for the workshop. And so, AWE was born: Affirming, Welcoming, and Engaging People in Your Catholic Parish. Today, there is a People Engagement Office (AWE) and special place on the St. Lad's website that exclusively deals with and explains the

AWE process—especially as it continues years after the original workshops.

So, what is AWE all about? It is best summarized by what Saint John Paul II said, "Today, in particular, the pressing pastoral task of the new evangelization calls for the involvement of the entire people of God, and requires a new fervor, new methods and a new expression for the announcing and witnessing of the Gospel." Affirm. Welcome. Engage.

If we believe that development is the meaningful involvement of people, and if we believe in the 7 "I"s of Identify-Inform-Invite-Involve-Implement-Invest-Improve, and if we understand that the best way to develop our parish is through people engagement and having the processes to make that happen, then we are ready to make those three words come alive. Part III of this book will lay out the process where AWE can come alive, and we will go through and explain each of the steps:

1. Create the organizational structure for Catholic Parish Development;
2. Create the core team;
3. Assess your Catholic parish development/stewardship efforts;
4. Seek input from your parishioners;
5. Create/affirm your parish mission and vision;
6. Create the strategic plan to address your parish's challenges;
7. Personally invite people using the 60% (uninvolved/new)—40% (involved) rule;
8. Write the strategic plan for parish development;
9. "Hire" the parish development/stewardship director;
10. Implement the best strategic solutions.

Using best practices and specific examples, I would like to share two stories—one from St. Ladislas Parish in Westlake, Ohio, and one from Our Lady of Lourdes Parish in Slidell, Louisiana.

ST. LADISLAS PARISH

Several years ago, Bud Teztlaff sent me a summary of how the parish had been doing in their first two years of implementing the AWE process.

The statistics are frightening: church membership is declining; there are fewer priests, and we have an aging clergy. In a typical Catholic parish, 30% are actively engaged, 30% are uninvolved, and 40% are actively disengaged. That means 70% of the parishioners are not involved or engaged in the life of the parish. It is truly a crisis. What can we do? No, what *must* be done—now?

The answer came in the AWE process, which is an acronym for Affirming, Welcoming and Engaging. AWE has become a compass, a rudder, and a way of life at St. Ladislas Parish on the west side of Cleveland, Ohio. Our pastor, Father Donald Snyder, calls it "a paradigm shift that we as a parish are committed to for the long term." We are doing strategic planning in a church. We ask ourselves at every turn or decision: will this create engagement? We firmly believe that *belonging leads to believing*. People come to church today for many reasons. It is up to the parish leaders to nurture our parishioners' sense of belonging and emotional commitment, as well as to make them feel not just welcomed, but also wanted and valued.

Our journey began in 2012 when our pastor and a few others evaluated the Institute for School and Parish Development's AWE workshop series. In early 2013, we committed ourselves to the year-long training program with other neighboring parishes. After organizing our core team, we conducted a survey of over 800 members of our parish. The results were quite revealing. At first, we thought we were doing well but knew there was room for improvement. After further analysis, we realized we mostly received surveys from the 30% who attend Mass regularly, so responses were biased. Moving forward, we discovered the real challenge was how to engage the 70% of our parish that is uninvolved or disengaged. We randomly invited parishioners who were largely disengaged to meetings to ask them how we could be more engaging. Surprisingly, people showed up and provided valuable input in these small-group sessions. We then organized several *people engagement teams* that met three times to sort through all the suggestions and data; from there we developed a plan of action. Throughout this process, the absolute key to success was the unwavering commitment by our pastor. Without that commitment, the process would have been a fancy-named program that would have faded over time and not made meaningful change happen within the fabric of the parish.

By the end of 2013, we had identified five key challenges and, under each challenge, four or five strategies or action ideas to help accomplish that specific challenge.

Now the real work began. The implementation of the specific strategies identified was to be the real measure of success. Execution is so critical. Below are a handful of the many new initiatives, ministries, or programs started over the last year and a half:

- Revised our sign-up form for our annual parish fair, which helped discern one's gifts and talents;
- Revamped our new-parishioner-welcome procedure to include a personal invitation to get involved in the church early on, and a new-parishioner dinner;
- Started a parishioner spotlight section in the bulletin to recognize parishioner accomplishments;
- Created an engagement office within the parish offices;
- Started "Name Tag Sunday," so now when we greet someone we can do so by first name;
- Expanded the Sunday socials—coffee and donuts—from a few times a year to almost every weekend after each Sunday Mass;
- Created a phone ministry, called "Father's Phoners," where we call every parishioner four times a year to personally invite them to special events at church;

- Created a team to expand our information technology to improve communications;
- Installed a state-of-the-art system to live-stream live Mass or other functions at church over the internet;
- Restarted a quarterly parish newsletter to be mailed and e-mailed to all parishioners;
- Developed several new social events with the goal to create engagement;
- Revised our parish website to be more user friendly;
- Began "Spiritual Nights" with different ministries that allow groups to gather with a sense of reflection on how their involvement is deepening their faith journey;
- Changed the parish picnic time and venue to be more "kid" and family friendly;
- Began an annual "Advent Tree Lighting Ceremony" with the Good Shepherd school children and all parishioners to mark the start of Advent and create a family tradition;
- Revamped our registration phone and staff welcoming process to include a new data form, a photograph of the family and a follow-up letter from the pastor;
- Began mailing welcome letters from the parish to new residents of Westlake to promote membership at our church;
- Developed the "No Souls Left Behind" initiative whereby, through random phone calls, parishioners are invited to share their need for prayers for those not attending church, for mothers and fathers, or for any concern for which they want the parish to pray;
- Developed a "Moms" group with an outreach to new mothers, which includes a periodic dinner;
- Began a series of quarterly training meetings with the ushers and greeters to discuss welcoming practices and procedures;
- Started a new process to assist parish leaders in integrating new members, succession planning, and empowering members.

So, how are we doing today? At a recent new parishioner welcoming dinner, one new parishioner said, "St. Ladislas is one of the best kept secrets." No, we do not want to be a "secret." That's a challenge in itself. But it is being "one of the best" that may tell it all. Membership is increasing. Volunteer signups for the over 60 ministries or groups is up over 10% from last year. New ministries are being created. Church attendance and financial support are improving. St. Ladislas is becoming a more dynamic and vibrant parish, one disengaged parishioner at a time, thanks to its unwavering focus on "belonging leads to believing" and the AWE process.

In May 2018, I received an e-mail from Bud, who shared some metrics that they feel have shown the positive effect of the AWE process.

- Since 2013, we had 10%–15% growth per year in parishioners signing up in various ministries. A true measure of engagement.
- Registrations are tracked, database cleaned up, resulting in new parishioner growth of 5%–10% per year.
- St. Ladislas was one of the first in the Diocese of Cleveland to stream live Masses, weddings, funerals, and baptisms.
- Our recent parish survey indicated significant improvement in all areas, especially welcoming and engagement. We added a new question to the recent survey that asked if parishioners would recommend St. Lads; 97% agreed.
- The pastor is totally committed to the AWE process; it is now "part of our DNA."
- For our Lenten mission this year, we hand-delivered a book to every disengaged parishioner/family, which was close to 50% (versus 70% nationally) of our parish.

OUR LADY OF LOURDES PARISH

In the mid-1990s, my family moved to Slidell, Louisiana, where we became members of Our Lady of Lourdes, a parish that can trace its beginnings back to 1890. At that time, I was busy with ISPD and traveling all over the country, my wife was holding down a job at a hospital, and we were expecting our first child. Because of our schedules, neither of us were motivated to step forward without an invitation, and so for a number of years we were that registered and regular parish family that attended Mass on the weekends and then went home.

Father Adrian Hall took over as pastor in 2002. I had worked with Father Hall when he was the pastor at a neighboring parish, so he was aware of ISPD and the work we do. When he found out that we were parishioners, I remember his phone call: "Frank, I really need your help here at Our Lady of Lourdes, and I hope because you and your family are parishioners here, this will be your gift of total stewardship."

Father Hall knew how to state his position. And so, in 2002, ISPD began to work with the parish. It was a wonderful journey. At the time Father Hall took over, there were approximately 2,200 families, an excellent socioeconomic mixture of people, and a strong base of families who made up the backbone of the parish in terms of their dedication, commitment, and love of their faith. Approximately 200 families were actively involved in ministries; 500+ were identified offertory givers (IOGs) with weekly collections around $7,400; there was no long-range plan in place; the school had a mandatory bingo for school parents to serve; parishioners, like those in many Catholic parishes, migrated to those people with whom they were familiar—family members, neighbors, and life-long friends. While I am sure there were new initiatives that were being explored before Father Hall arrived, we never were aware of a dynamic vision for the future of the parish. As time would tell, that vision would be forced on the people of OLL.

From September 2002 until August 2005, we worked with

Father Hall and parish leaders and followed the steps for parish development:

- Formation of a core team;
- Education of parish leaders on the value of Catholic Parish Development;
- Assessment of parish development and stewardship efforts;
- Parish-wide survey;
- Establishment of a development office with a parish/school development director;
- Identification of challenges, as seen in the survey results;
- Strategic action initiatives to solve the main challenges;
- Implementation of a total stewardship process of prayer, service, and finance;
- Establishment of a people engagement culture.

As will be covered in detail in later lessons, these steps proved to be very successful. By August 2005, there were 200–300 new families who had become involved in ministries and activities. More than 800 families were on track to participate in stewardship of prayer and/or stewardship of ministry and/or stewardship of finance. Weekly collections climbed to $14,000+ per week; a vision plan was created; input was sought and welcomed; everyone in the parish was personally invited to "belong" at least twice per year; neighborhood communities were being formed; and a new culture was being born, which was built from the wonderful people who had formed the fabric of the parish for many, many years.

On August 29, 2005, Hurricane Katrina came roaring in.

Our Lady of Lourdes was one of the hardest-hit parishes in the Archdiocese of New Orleans. The church was totally destroyed; the rectory was uninhabitable; the school had four feet of marsh water and "sludge" in every room; the gym was heavily damaged; the cafeteria was the only facility that could be salvaged. Immediately after Katrina left the Slidell area, Sunday Mass was celebrated at the street corner where the church was destroyed;

the gym provided a place of worship for the next few months; and eventually the cafeteria became the place where we worshiped for the next two to three years. Father Hall guided the parish through the first year of major change, and he then retired after many years of service. The archdiocese sent two priests, who moved the parish forward through full recovery—Father Frank Lipps and Father Kyle Dave. They ultimately transformed the parish facilities into what they are today—a new church in a new location on campus, a new school, cafeteria, and gym, and a remodeled rectory. The dedication of these two priests, a wonderful parish staff, and the commitment of parish families were all outstanding.

After Katrina hit, the parish went from 2,200 families to 800. People scattered to the four corners of the country and beyond. With all of the devastation, some parishes would have either closed down or taken years and years to rebuild. On May 15, 2010— less than five years from when Hurricane Katrina came roaring ashore—the new church at Our Lady of Lourdes was dedicated by Archbishop Gregory Aymond. In retrospect, I believe there are five reasons that made this possible:

- The leadership of Father Frank Lipps and Father Kyle Dave was all about engaging people;
- The past parish development/stewardship efforts (pre-Katrina), led by Father Adrian Hall, paved the way for better communication, better stewardship of finance, and better involvement opportunities;
- Our Lady of Lourdes Parish had 15–20 core families who formed the backbone of the parish and were instrumental in "staying the course";
- The parish development efforts rippled out to invite and involve hundreds of new people who moved into the parish, resulting in over 1,000 people who gave gifts of prayer, gifts of service, and gifts of financial participation to the capital campaign that kicked off two years after Hurricane Katrina—and went over its goal;

- AWE—Affirming, Welcoming, and Engaging—was alive during those years.

Questions, Exercises, and Next Best Steps for Lesson Three

1. What areas of your parish can you name where you could say that the parish staff, parish leaders (councils and advisory groups), ministry leaders, and parishioners in general are affirmed and appreciated? Please explain.

2. How important is affirmation to the overall culture of your parish? Please explain.

3. How are visitors to your parish welcomed on a week-to-week basis? Please explain.

4. How are new families welcomed into the parish? In the welcoming process, what ways are they meant to feel special and to feel like they belong? Please explain.

5. In your parish, what does the word "engagement" mean to you and your parish leaders? Please explain.

6. How does a people-engagement culture come alive in your parish? Please explain.

7. After reading and discussing this lesson, how would you rate the AWE level in your parish? _____

   5—Very high. All parish leaders (clergy, parish staff, councils, ministry leaders, etc.) are totally tuned into and implementing an affirming, welcoming, and engaging culture.

   4—High. All parish leaders understand the value and are taking the steps to implement this type of culture.

3—Some parish leaders understand the value of this kinds of culture, but we do not have any major steps in motion.

2—Some parish leaders are aware of this AWE culture, but nothing is being done.

1—Parish leaders have been doing things a set way for so long that ideas like an integrated AWE culture would not even be thought of as being necessary.

Lesson Four: Encourage Pastors to Take the Lead Role in Parish Development

|| "I can do things you cannot, you can do things I cannot; together we can do great things." MOTHER TERESA

Since 1989, we have had the opportunity to work with a number of pastors and other parish leaders. Most of the consults and workshops have been on how to organize and implement a vibrant Catholic Parish Development effort and/or how to introduce and integrate a successful stewardship plan of action. Inevitably, the question comes up from most pastors, "What is my role in all of these development efforts?" Overall, we have always said that the pastor's role is to work with the lay leaders of the parish and create a positive synergy that will become contagious.

Here are five points we recommend for pastors to consider.

RECOMMENDATION #1: INTRODUCE THE IMPORTANCE AND AFFIRM. (INTRODUCE)

- There are many parishioners who do not understand the importance of a vibrant and formal development effort in their parish. They see it mainly as fund-raising. When pastors and parish leaders believe in people engagement, they are

ready to introduce the concept that in order to develop
and advance their parish, all people need to be on board
as ambassadors and stewards. This should be a consistent
message.

- When parishioners hear the pastor speak about the new
parishioner welcome process and how well it is going, they
too understand the value of Catholic Parish Development.
- Pastors should constantly emphasize the importance
of Catholic Parish Development and select those many
opportunities to affirm and communicate the importance of
having that effort in place in their parish.

**RECOMMENDATION #2: HELP SET UP ORGANIZATIONAL
STRUCTURE AND PRIORITIES. (SET-UP)**

- The overall organization and structure of development
should be articulated by the pastor. Here at ISPD, we believe
in an organizational structure for parish development that is
presented and explained in Lesson Six.
- We believe in having a person in charge of the development
effort. This could be volunteer, part time, or full time. We also
believe in the core team concept of 15–18 leaders working
alongside the person in charge of development/stewardship
(Lesson Seven).
- With Catholic Parish Development, we believe in centering
the efforts around six areas:
  » Constituent records
  » Fund development
  » Total stewardship process
  » People engagement
  » Communications
  » Special events
- We recommend that the pastor help set up this organizational
structure with prioritized strategic initiatives.

RECOMMENDATION #3: MACRO-MANAGE THE EFFORT. (MACRO-MANAGE)

- Once the structure is in place, the pastor needs to macro-manage the progress, not micromanage. They should not be the implementers. This should be left up to the person(s) in charge of development and the core team.
- This is possibly the biggest shift in thinking for many pastors. Once priorities have been set, we recommend that pastors oversee, affirm, and let progress take place.

RECOMMENDATION #4: FOCUS ON PEOPLE ENGAGEMENT WITH SPECIAL ATTENTION TO PEOPLE WHO CAN MAKE A DIFFERENCE. (FOCUS)

- People want to be invited by the person in charge. It will be important for the pastor to, over time, develop a list of *parishioners who can make a difference* in their parish. These may be people with special gifts and talents, people with political connections, people who have strong financial capability, people who own their own business or serve in executive positions in corporations, people who can help identify leaders in the community, etc. The focus should be on inviting and involving them into the life of that Catholic institution.
- Every parish has people who want to make a difference. Ninety percent of the time they will not be the ones who raise their hands and step up; they need the door to be opened for them. The pastor can open that door and wonderful relationships can begin.
- We recommend that pastors schedule 5–6 personal visits (cup of coffee meeting) per month and have ongoing conversations with those people who can make a difference.

RECOMMENDATION #5: MONITOR MONTHLY AND ASSESS ANNUALLY. (ASSESS)

- As the overseer and macro-manager of the effort, it will be important for the pastor to monitor the development efforts on a monthly basis.
- In June of every year, we recommend that the overall development efforts be evaluated. (Please see Lesson Eight.)

Introduce, *Set-Up*, *Macro-Manage*, *Focus*, and *Assess* are what we recommend to pastors. There are numerous success stories throughout the country where these five recommendations continue to produce wonderful results in parishes.

CONVERSATION WITH A PASTOR

I would like to share a conversation that I had with a pastor; I believe the value of this lesson is best illustrated through this phone call. Although we have never worked together, I have known this pastor for a number of years. He has attended one or two of our workshops and in principle understands the true meaning of Catholic Parish Development. It was an interesting conversation, because he was facing a crisis in his parish unlike anything he had ever had to deal with. As he said, "They sure didn't teach us too much about all of this when I was in the seminary." Let's listen in.

"Father Dan, so good to hear from you," I said. "How is life in the cold northeast?"

"Well, we're at twelve degrees and falling—both literally and figuratively. But, I'm sure we're no worse off than anybody else, Frank. How are the good folks at ISPD? Still battling those seventy-degree temperatures in December?" he inquired.

"We're doing fine, Father. Everybody you met when you were down here in New Orleans for the ISPD workshop is still on board, and we're working with some challenging parishes," I answered.

"Frank," Father Dan said, "let me see if I can pick your brain a little bit, if you have the time. I've been at this parish now for three years. Nice place. People are friendly. About 1,400 families. Your rule of 30–30–40 is alive and well. About 30% of our families are involved, 30% are not involved, and 40% are just out there—names are in the database. Child needed to be baptized; daughter needed to be married; spouse needed to be buried. You know how it is. Good people, but it's hard to get them engaged. Same ones doing the same thing. And everyone is busy."

"Well, Father, knowing you, you probably have tried a bunch of new ideas—new programs, new ministries. You were always good at creating," I responded.

"Yes, I did and still do, but nothing dramatically has changed, and now with the economy the way it is, things have only gotten worse. Job layoffs, weekend collections way off, school tuition payments late. I spend a lot of my time trying to make judgment calls without being too harsh with people. It does take money to run this place, you know."

"Father, obviously, you've got some real challenges. Tell me, over the past year what kinds of things have you been doing?"

"Well, we've tried a bunch of things," he said. "I've written letters to all of the parish families and let them know where we stand. I've spoken from the pulpit several times about our financial situation. Back six months ago, we hired a company to come in and write a series of letters to our parishioners asking them to increase their giving or, if they weren't doing anything, to please consider it. One letter right after the other, and although we saw a positive blip on the books, after four months, we were back to where we started. No real foundation of people."

"Father, as you know," I said, "that's the key. We seem to get so good at mailing and e-mailing and talking from the pulpit and putting great stuff on our website and putting things in the bulletin and sending out e-mails and asking people to sign up for this and that, and yet we don't seem to take the time to talk to folks—eyeball to eyeball."

"Frank, I agree," he stated. "It seems the only chances I have to interact with people are after Mass, at staff meetings, when I visit folks in the hospital, and when I meet with families for baptisms and funerals and weddings. Any suggestions?"

"Well, the first thing is to realize, as you know, that the heart of Catholic Parish Development is building relationships. It is so hard to do this because it does take time. Yet the first step is to build a culture that is inviting, hospitable, welcoming, affirming, and engaging. Father, sometimes I am reluctant to say this, but it all starts and is continuously supported by you. You don't have to cook the meal, but you certainly do have to serve it."

"What do you mean by that, Frank?" Father asked.

"Father, you set the tone for whether or not the parish is warm, lukewarm, or cold. You establish that atmosphere where people feel like they belong and want to keep coming back. You do it from the pulpit; you do it by picking up the phone ten times per month and calling families that you don't know but who are registered as parishioners in your parish. You get your pastoral council members to do the same—by calling ten families each month and saying hi. You do it by proclaiming at your key ministry meetings that 'warmth' is the theme of the parish, and everyone needs to get on board. You do it by launching a vibrant greeters' ministry or by holding three or four town hall meetings every year and just opening up the floor to talk and invite input. You do it by hosting a pastor breakfast once a month and inviting ten parishioner families whom you don't know very well. You do it by creating an action plan for people engagement and inviting fifty or more people to help you come up with action strategies to make it all come alive. You do it by personally visiting four or five families in their home each month and having a cup of coffee. You do it by getting others to "buy into" this way of thinking on how to build church. You do it by hosting "Bring a Friend" Sundays three or four times per year where you invite your parishioners to bring a friend to celebrate liturgy. You do it by surveying your people at least once a year and asking their opinion—at Mass, online, through the mail, or any other way you can get their best wisdom. You do it by having the parish host a family night once or twice a month and having movies and games and sports and hamburgers and hot dogs. You do it by always remembering that 'belonging does lead to believing.'"

"Frank, that sure sounds like a lot of work. I am soooo busy. How can I do all of this?" Father Dan inquired.

"Father, two things," I replied. "First of all, you cannot do all of this by yourself, but you've got to set the tone, and you've got to take the first steps. These are first steps that have never been done before, such as making five to ten phone calls every month to say hi. Can you imagine the impact this will have? In those parishes where the pastors took the time to do this, most people respond by saying, 'I can't believe Father took the time to call me.' Second, you've got to answer the question: How important is all of this to your parish? If you truly believe that people are the answer—and here at ISPD we do—then you will take the time to make this happen. I know it seems like a lot, but look at the possibilities. People are craving relationships and to feel a strong sense of belonging. That is what we can do in the Catholic Church—we can give people hope; we can show people the way to come in and make a difference; we can invite people to belong. But you know what, Father? In our experience that just ain't gonna happen by sending them another letter asking for more money, or standing up in the pulpit and saying how bad things are, or inviting people to come to the Lord's table and not making them feel welcome, warm, and needed."

"That's a tall order, Frank."

"Yes, Father, it certainly is, but what is exciting is what can happen when a parish places the emphasis on building a stronger faith community through people engagement. People simply love to belong, and that tone is set by our leaders. And the greatest news is that this all works, and you will be great at moving this forward at your parish. It can be done, and I have no doubt that you can set the tone and establish the pace. It is all about bringing people to Christ, and Christ to people. And you are so good at that. But it starts with a handshake, or a phone call, or simple personal invitation. And, Father, remember those weddings and funerals and baptisms you spoke about? Those are all entry points for many families to get to know you and others in the parish. Select 1–2 people and invite them for coffee to just get to know them. The results are nothing short of amazing. Father, you can do this. Please keep me posted. God bless."

Questions, Exercises, and Next Best Steps for Lesson Four

1. How well does the pastor of your parish understand Catholic Parish Development and the value of engaging people? Please explain.

2. Does your parish have any kind of parish development office in place with someone in charge? Please explain.

3. Based on what you have learned in these early lessons, how difficult would it be to organize and implement a vibrant parish development effort in your parish? Please explain.

4. Does your parish have the leadership (pastor, associate pastor, parish council member, ministry leader, etc.) who can clearly articulate the value of Catholic Parish Development from the pulpit? Please explain.

5. In your opinion, is there any way that Catholic Parish Development can flourish without the pastor's full support? ☐ Yes ☐ No Please explain.

6. If your parish has a pastor who does not understand Catholic

Parish Development, what steps would you suggest to get him on board? Please explain.

7. In 250 words or fewer, write a presentation from the pulpit in which a parish leader would introduce Catholic Parish Development to all parishioners at one of your Masses.

Lesson Five: Understand What Makes an "Alive" and "Warm" Catholic Parish

> "The parish is not an outdated institution; precisely because it possesses great flexibility, it can assume quite different contours depending on the openness and missionary creativity of the pastor and the community." POPE FRANCIS

Throughout my years as a Catholic development consultant, I have had the wonderful opportunity to celebrate liturgy in parishes all over the country—with wonderful pastors and engaging parishioners. Sometimes these were special Masses, such as during a kick-off reception or special event, and other times these were weekend Masses in a parish where I was working. Attending Mass at over 150 different parishes since 1989, I have come to appreciate the difference between a "warm" parish and a "cold" parish. Most of the time, I could tell the difference within five minutes.

Several years ago, I was asked at a workshop what makes certain parishes warm and engaging and others cold and "standoffish." It was a wonderful question, and for the next month or so, I wrote down those positive traits from those exceptionally warm parishes I had visited. It was an interesting exercise, and after going over these attributes with the ISPD staff, I was encouraged to create a story that is now called, "The *Warm* Catholic Parish." I would like to share this with you.

THE "WARM" CATHOLIC PARISH

Ray and Michelle (ages 34 and 32) and their two small children, ages 5 and 7, move to Anytown, USA. They are a Catholic family looking for a parish to join; they want what they call the "perfect fit." Their neighbor tells them that there is a Catholic church a couple of miles away, and so they decide to check on Mass times, and they end up attending 10:30 AM Mass that Sunday.

When they arrive on Sunday, there are signs showing them where to park. As they walk toward the entrance of the church, people from the parish are there to greet them and wish them "Good morning!" They walk into a well-lit, large gathering space where they are once again greeted and welcomed—as if they had been going to 10:30 Mass there every Sunday.

The usher closest to them directs them to a pew and hands them booklets to use, which have the hymns and the readings. The usher also explains that before the readings, children are invited to participate in "Children's Liturgy of the Word." He tells that to all families with children. As Ray and Michelle and their children settle in, they notice two large screens on either side of the altar.

At 10:20, the music director, exuding energy and encouragement and referring to the two large screens that display the verses and chorus of each hymn, goes over the music for the Mass with the congregation.

At 10:25, the lector reads the announcements, and at 10:30 the Mass begins with the processional song, played with wonderful instrumentation and the entire congregation singing as they watch the words scroll down on the two screens.

After the opening hymn, the priest invites all to worship—a genuine invitation to come into the holy presence of the Lord.

Before the first reading, the priest invites all children under 15 to participate in the "Children's Liturgy of the Word," and he blesses them as they leave the church and move into an adjacent building with classrooms.

Before the first and second readings, the priest explains what the congregation needs to listen for in each reading and what key messages they can anticipate. Both readings are displayed on the two large screens for everyone to read along.

After the gospel, the priest engages the entire church with an inspiring and meaningful homily that lasts for five minutes. After the homily, the children reenter, smiling and excited because of the excellent experience of their "Liturgy of the Word."

With the offertory, the priest explains the many gifts that are brought forward, and as he prepares all for the body and blood of Christ, there is soft music in the background that adds "color" and "dimension" to his words.

Within the Communion Rite, the sign of peace takes place; Christ's peace brings people into union, into communion—a meaningful symbol that is not lost on Ray and Michelle.

As people receive communion, in an organized manner, the choir sings in the background, and after communion, no one leaves church.

Before the final blessing, the priest invites all to sit, and he takes the time to welcome all new parish families that month, calling them out by family name—whether they are there or not. He welcomes all newcomers and visitors and expresses his joy at them being there to worship. He then refers to the parish connection cards that are in each pew; he points out that these cards are for all people present—parishioners, guests, friends, or visitors. He invites them to fill in the card if they wish to connect—to him, to a ministry, to a staff member. He explains that the connection may be a request or a question or a need or simply a desire for more information. He invites all people who fill in a connection card to hand it to one of the hospitality ministers on their way out of Mass or to drop it in one of the large baskets by each of the entrance/exit doors of the church.

He then invites all to have a wonderful week and takes the time to commend a special ministry or group of people in the parish. He sends people on their way with a smile as he thanks the many people who made this liturgical celebration possible.

As Ray and Michelle and their children leave, they are greeted by one of the hospitality ministers, who hands them the weekly bulletin and thanks them for coming to worship. They also hand in the connection card they had filled out.

Once in their car, the family cannot stop talking about how welcome they had felt and how warm of a reception they had received. They mention that they not only filled in a card but also received the bulletin with information on who, when, and where to call if they need further information.

On Monday, Michelle calls the parish office to register and gives basic information to the person known as the "parish involvement director." This person also lets Michelle know that the pastor will be calling within the next week. On Thursday, they receive a call from the pastor, who welcomes them to the parish and also invites them to a reception on a given date. The pastor also lets them know that two people from the hospitality ministry will be calling to set up an appointment in order to bring them information about the parish and talk with them about their needs. The following week, Ray and Michelle receive a phone call from Steve and Barb, who schedule a time to come to their home.

During the first half of the visit, Steve and Barb go over the ministries of the parish; they talk about stewardship of prayer, ministry, and offering. They give them the parish handbook and also a basket of baked goodies. After explaining many things about the parish and answering questions, Steve and Barb then say, "Ray and Michelle, please share with us what your needs are. What is it that you think is important for us to know about you and your family as new members of our faith community?"

After that engaging conversation, Ray and Michelle are asked what it is they do best—what gifts and talents they would like to share as stewards of the parish. They both talk about what they enjoy doing—how Ray likes to facilitate meetings and how he enjoys showing people how to set up a household budget. Michelle talks about her public relations skills, how she enjoys writing, and how she likes to organize special events. Steve and Barb capture all of that information, plus more, and they also get their e-mail addresses and cell phone numbers.

Before they leave, Steve and Barb remind Ray and Michelle of four things: 1. to remember the reception hosted by the pastor; 2. to look over the many ministries of the parish; 3. to consider the different religious education opportunities; and, 4. to think of ways they could use their gifts in the parish. Steve and Barb also schedule a follow-up meeting after the pastor's reception.

Ray and Michelle receive a follow-up phone call from the pastor's assistant three days before the reception. When they arrive at the reception, they are introduced to four other new families. They talk about themselves, listen to what others have to say about themselves, and then share evening prayer and a meal together. As they leave, the pastor thanks them for a wonderful evening and invites them all to consider being part of an "affinity group" in the future. He explains that this will be a group of 8–10 families (mostly new) who will get together six times a year and share a meal, prayer, and stories of their families. He or one of the parish leaders will always be present with update news.

At the follow-up visit a couple of weeks later, Steve and Barb discuss the ministries and what Ray and Michelle would like to do. They ask them how they would like to share their gifts in the parish. They discuss the prayer opportunities and mention to both of them the different kinds of retreats that they encourage each family to experience at least once per year. They also talk with Ray and Michelle about the many opportunities for their children— both in terms of fun activities as well as spiritual growth.

They go over their intention card, which invites them to be a steward of the parish. Ray and Michelle are invited to fill the card in over the next week or so. The card invites gifts of prayer, ministry, and offering. They also leave Ray and Michelle with the Sunday offertory giving envelopes and explain what that money is used for. They then ask Ray and Michelle if they had thought about being part of an affinity group. When they say yes, Steve and Barb share with them the details about their first "pot luck" dinner and who will be there.

Over the next several days, Ray and Michelle and their children discuss their initial experience in the parish. They all agree that they have found a home and look forward to being active stewards in the life of the parish. Their journey and experience at this Catholic parish has begun—in a personal way.

Questions, Exercises, and Next Best Steps for Lesson Five

1. Based on the description above, would you say your parish is "warm" or "cold"? Please explain.

2. How does your parish receive communication from parishioners and visitors about any needs they may have? Please explain.

3. How much value does your parish place on personally getting to know new parish families? Please explain.

4. How "far-fetched" or unrealistic is the fictional story of Ray and Michelle told in this lesson? Please explain.

5. What creative ways can you think of for new parish families to connect with those families in your parish who have been there for many years? Please describe.

PART III

Processes and Structures to Develop and Advance Your Catholic Parish

Lesson Six: Create the Organizational Structure for Catholic Parish Development Success

‖ Commit your work to the Lord, and your plans will be established. PROVERBS 16:3

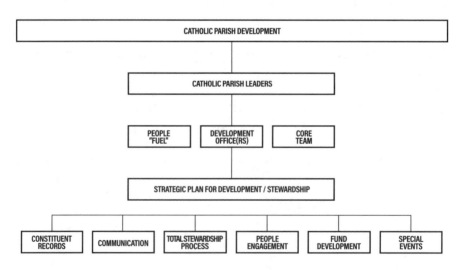

"Back in the day," as folks often say, very few Catholic parishes gave much thought to setting up an organizational structure for development. Parishes focused on stewardship, and offertory collections pretty much defined what stewardship was focused on.

Even today, this remains true for many parishes, as shown in their Sunday bulletins where the "Stewardship Corner" is all about how much money was collected the previous weekend and whether or not collections are on track to meet the demands of the budget.

However, there are those Catholic parishes who see development and stewardship as much more than putting on a parish fair, or mailing out offertory envelopes, or hiring a fund-raising company to come in and write fund-raising letters, or having a welcoming committee in the parish, or having a page on Facebook. While these specific strategic initiatives can be successful, and many people in charge of these activities do implement them from year to year, there is a major challenge: How do all of these dots connect? How can this series of activities be organized and understood by the many constituents of a Catholic parish?

The organizational diagram on page 46 shows the main components for a Catholic Parish Development effort. Let's look at these and provide a brief description:

1. Constituent Records: This important area is all about keeping track of the people who make up your parish. As we always say, "A Catholic Parish Development effort is only as good as its ability to keep track of its constituents (parishioners, visitors, ministry leaders, donors, media sources, etc.)." This is your database.

2. Communication: This is such an important area. The person handling communication is responsible for public relations, marketing, design, and copy—from direct mail to the website to press releases to e-mails to newsletters to annual reports to weekly bulletins to social media to photography to special invitations to literature for special events, etc. This is the area that informs people what has gone on, what is going on, and what will go on in your parish.

3. Total Stewardship Process: This is the area that works closely with people engagement and with fund development and invites people to share their gifts of prayer, service, and finance.

4. People Engagement: This is the area in parish development that seeks to address the great challenge for Catholic parishes throughout the country—the challenge to engage the 70% of people who are "uninvolved" or "actively disengaged," as Gallup refers to them.

5. Fund Development: Seen in the diagram, fund development points to those processes that invite people to invest—philanthropic giving. It is the parish annual fund, the capital campaign, major donor invitations, planned giving, endowed giving, and memorial giving.

6. Special Fund/Friend-Raising Events and Activities: This area involves the special events of the parish. Events such as the fair, the golf tournament, the poinsettia sale, the parish assembly, the bishop's reception—all events that are meant to either fund-raise and/or friend-raise.

As we have said numerous times, we invite people to view Catholic development in terms of a system of processes—all centered around these major areas or components and all Catholic leaders understanding the 7 "I"s of Identify-Inform-Invite-Involve-Implement-Invest-Improve.

The 7 "I"s of Catholic Parish Development

Questions, Exercises, and Next Best Steps for Lesson Six

As seen in this lesson, there are six major components of an active Catholic parish development system:

- Constituent relations (database)

- Communications

- Total stewardship process (prayer, service, and finance)

- People engagement

- Fund development
  - » Parish annual fund
  - » Parish capital campaign
  - » Planned giving
  - » Memorial giving
  - » Endowed giving
  - » Major donor invitations

- Special fund/friend-raising events and activities

In your parish, what is presently in place in these six areas?

- Constituent relations (database management)

- Communications

- Total stewardship process (prayer, service, and finance)

- People engagement (active effort to engage people)

- Fund development (annual fund, capital campaign, planned giving, memorial giving, major donor work)

- Special fund/friend-raising events and activities

Lesson Seven: Create the Parish Development Core Team

> "Never doubt that a small group of thoughtful and committed people can change the world. Indeed, it is the only thing that ever has." MARGARET MEAD

In previous lessons, we have talked about the importance of the "core team." This group can become the most valuable addition to a Catholic parish development effort, if we understand what their role is and how they can relate to the overall formation of a quality development process.

Years ago, I was conducting a two-day development workshop in the Diocese of San Jose. At the end of the first day, a pastor approached me; he had an excellent perspective. He said, "Mr. Donaldson, everything you are talking about certainly makes sense. But who is going to do all of this stewardship work? We cannot afford a development director, and I certainly do not have the time to do it. What are your suggestions?"

This was a great question, and one to which I did not have an immediate answer. However, over the next few months, we brainstormed ideas here at the company and eventually came up with one of the most practical suggestions since we opened the doors in 1989: the parish development core team.

This is a "roll up your sleeves" group that becomes the "right arm" of the development operation. We will explain this by way of a Q & A format.

What is the core team in a parish development effort?

The core team that works with the development efforts of a parish is a group of 15–18 dedicated and committed people who create, implement, and sustain the development processes. The initial thrust is toward the following:

- Deciding on the need and rationale for Catholic Parish Development

- Assuring the commitment level

- Understanding Catholic Parish Development

- 7 "I" approach

- Introducing development to the parish community

- Identifying the development challenges the parish faces

- Conducting input sessions with parish families

The major focus of the core team is to work closely with the pastor and, if there are personnel in place, to work with the development officer(s). The real value of the core team is serving as the implementers of the plans that are created. They guide and direct these processes.

Who should be on the parish development core team?

The people who serve on the core team should come from the "first ripple out." They are usually inner-circle members already and leaders in the parish. They must be positive, mission-driven individuals who strongly believe in the parish and where it is going. They should be able to work in a team setting and be true team players. At least half of the members should be able to speak well in front of a small or large group of people—especially as this applies to teaching others what development is all about. Besides the pastor, who is an ex-officio member, you could have representation from:

- parish staff
- parish council

- finance council
- ministry leaders

- school leaders (if applicable)
- key donor(s)—actual/potential

After the initial meeting, it may be necessary to add or amend the original list in order to get good representation. It will be important to have the names, addresses, phone numbers, and e-mail addresses of the members of this team so they can stay informed every step of the way.

What are their roles and responsibilities?

- To serve as the "steering wheel" to the development process, to help decide what needs to be done and then do it;

- To provide background information and any historical perspective that may be needed as the parish moves through the development process;

- To identify people in the parish who will be asked to get involved in this effort;

- To help invite these people to become involved:
  » input sessions,
  » planning teams,
  » financial leaders;

- To serve as spokespersons for the development effort in case anyone in the parish wishes to find out more about it;

- To share any concern or issue that needs to be discussed before it may reach the problem stage out in the parish community;

- To honor the confidentiality of the information that is discussed in this core team—especially as it concerns other individual members of the parish community;

- To serve in leadership positions when asked to do so—for example, to help facilitate input sessions or small-group meetings;

- To offer news and bulletin information that would be pertinent to the development effort;

- To always remain positive and vision-driven.

Who selects and invites the core team members?

- The pastor "hand selects" these folks. He and any other key parish leader usually sit down and come up with a list of twenty people. Usually, these people are already leaders in the parish, and because this effort is so important, they need to be invited to step forward and possibly even drop something else with which they are working.

- The invitation is done one on one and should be extended by the pastor.

- Please understand that this is not a team that is open for membership to anyone. This is a carefully selected group who will roll up their sleeves and make things happen.

What are the keys to a successful core team?

We usually look for the following:

- Members who are committed—not just interested.

- Members who are on time for meetings.

- Meetings begin on time and end on time and are scheduled for months in advance.

- There is an agenda for each meeting.

- There is a report from each meeting with the results shared with team members before the next meeting.

- Team members respect each other's opinions—although they may not always agree on everything.

- The core team is geared toward four major areas:
  - » Helping guide and facilitate the development process,
  - » Offering key suggestions for success,

- » Helping implement key strategies,
- » Continuing to educate and inform all parish groups on what is going on with the development effort.

- All ideas are discussed out in the open, and conversations do not continue into the "parking lot" with hidden agendas. The core team must be solid and members must trust one another.

- The mission of the development core team should be created, and it must be clear to all.

What is the difference between the core team and the parish (pastoral) council?

Here are points to consider:

- The parish development core team focuses on the implementation of the six areas of parish development—constituent records, communications, total stewardship process, fund-development, people engagement, and fund/friend-raising events. Usually, two or three members of the parish council serve on the core team.

- An important point to understand is this: if a parish has a stewardship committee or council, this group usually cannot serve as the parish development core team simply because the core team does much more than just total stewardship. It is always a good idea to have two or three members of the stewardship committee/council on the parish development core team.

Questions, Exercises, and Next Best Steps for Lesson Seven

1. At this point in the book, and as you look at your Catholic Parish Development efforts, what are the top 6–8 challenges you presently face?

2. In your Catholic Parish Development efforts at the present time, are you using a core team of 15–18 people to assist with the development efforts of the parish? If yes, please explain how this team is used.

3. If you do not have a core team in place, what are the main areas of parish development that you would want a team to work with? Constituent relations? Communications? Total stewardship process? People engagement? Fund development? Special events?

4. In order of priority, write down the names of 25 people and what group(s) they represent (e.g., parish staff, ministry leader, parish council, stewardship council, school leader, etc.) that you would like to invite to be part of your Catholic parish core team:

   Name   Group(s) represented

5. After completing your list, send each person a letter, personally addressed and signed by the pastor. Three to five days after the letter has been put in the mail, have the pastor personally call and invite each person to be a member of the core team. Please refer to the sample letter on the following page.

Sample Core Team Invitation

Dear _____ ,

As we continue our journey of developing and advancing our unique mission here at (name of parish), we have entered into a Catholic Parish Development process that will allow us to continue to create a strong people-engagement culture in our parish—one where everyone will feel welcomed and will experience the belief that this is indeed their spiritual home.

One of the main leadership groups with whom we will be working will be the Parish Development Core Team. This group of 15 to 18 people will meet on a regular basis and help us not only to create but also to implement our strategic plan for development in a number of areas. Planning areas we are considering at this time are communications, people engagement, fund development, total stewardship, and special events.

I would like to personally invite you to become a member of the core team that will steer this process over the next twelve months. The first meeting is scheduled for _____ (date), at _____ (time) in the _____ (place).

Thank you so much for considering this important role in our parish's future. Indeed, these are exciting times being driven by leaders willing to set the pace and advance the mission of _____ for many years to come. We will be contacting you within the next week or so in order to discuss your involvement with this planning and implementation team.

Sincerely,
(Pastor)

Lesson Eight: Assess/Evaluate Your Catholic Parish Development Efforts

|| **"Without proper self-evaluation, failure is inevitable."**
|| JOHN WOODEN

Whether a parish has a vibrant development effort "up and running" or is just getting started with a more organized approach, there is great value in assessing what you are doing. Now that we have defined what development is, and before we move into further understanding and implementation, let's have you and your parish leaders assess how you are doing with your parish development efforts. Listed here in Lesson Eight are 145 statements to answer, and after taking this "test," parish leaders should be able to identify the strengths and weaknesses of their development efforts. Once again, one of the first steps in any development process is assessing where you are. This instrument should give you an excellent perspective. In addition, this is an excellent exercise for a parish development core team to work with.

True–False–Somewhat Test (TFS Test)

Please write **T** *if the statement is True for your parish,* **F** *if the statement is False for your parish, and* **S** *if the statement is neither all True nor all False. In other words, it is somewhat True and somewhat False. Please write* **NA** *for Not Applicable.*

NOTE

It is best to take the TFS test as a small group or committee, or have 8–10 people (or the core team) take it individually and then get together to compare answers and come up with a composite score.

   It is not best to have one person (pastor, total stewardship and development director, head of the stewardship committee, etc.) take the TFS test and only use that as the basis for assessment.

ASSESSMENT AREA #1:
CATHOLIC PARISH DEVELOPMENT PRINCIPLES

1. _____ Even though you may not have a formal effort in place (office, written plan, director, etc.), you do recognize the need for a formal development effort in your parish.

2. _____ Your internal publics (parish staff, finance council, parish council, etc.) understand that development is not just about raising money.

3. _____ The development effort is not being set up as a "smokescreen for money."

4. _____ You do realize that development is a whole new way of looking at things.

5. _____ One of the topics for discussion at your parish council and parish staff meetings is in the area of Catholic Parish Development.

6. _____ Your parish has a clear mission and vision statement that is shared with all key internal publics.

7. _____ Your parish does have a long-range, pastoral plan of some kind in place.

8. _____ Your ministries that meet the needs of your parish families are filled with quality people and excellent leaders.

9. _____ The pastor understands Catholic Parish Development and supports the efforts.

10. _____ Regarding the financial side of parish development, your parish leadership operates under the principle: "In order to make money, we've got to spend money."

11. _____ Your development effort is making progress year to year, and the yardstick of measurement is the following:

Invitation and involvement of people;

New approaches to old problems and situations;

Creativity;

Further understanding of the many gifts (skills, talents, wisdom, finances, time, etc.) your parishioners can bring.

12. _____ Your development effort concentrates heavily on engaging people.

13. _____ You are always looking to involve people from a win-win position by answering the question: What's in it for them?

14. _____ Your development effort is proactive, not reactive.

15. _____ Your development effort is done just as much person-to-person and in small groups rather than just on paper and through direct mail.

ASSESSMENT AREA #2:
CATHOLIC PARISH DEVELOPMENT ORGANIZATION AND STRUCTURE

16. _____ You continually gather information about your parish families and maintain an excellent database that lists their many gifts and talents and levels of expertise and wisdom.

17. _____ Your database is up-to-date on the following publics:

INTERNAL	EXTERNAL
Administration	*All parish families*
Parish staff	*New parishioners registered within*
Finance council	*the past six months*
Ministry leaders	*Education parents: school and parish*
Parish council	*Businesses who support your parish*
Commissions	*Media sources*

18. _____ Through personal conversations, fund-raising efforts, offertory giving, capital campaigns, and major gift work, you have been able to identify who is capable of being a financial leader.

19. _____ There is an organizational chart in place that shows the relationship of development to the other ministries and organizations of the parish.

20. _____ If applicable, there are clear job descriptions in place for those people working with the development efforts.

21. _____ Your Catholic Parish Development effort has one of the following configurations:
Full-time development director
Part-time development director
Volunteer development director or committee
Consultant and volunteers
Consultant and paid part-time or full-time development director
Catholic Parish Development core team

22. _____ You have a formal budget for the development efforts.

23. _____ You do see the value of this development assessment that can help you assess your situation, tell you what the strengths and weaknesses are, and then encourage you to make positive changes.

24. _____ If applicable, the development director (also possibly called the stewardship director) is considered part of the parish leadership team.

25. _____ The people involved and interested in development have attended one or more professional workshops in order to receive proper training in this field.

26. _____ You have begun to build a library of professional reading materials on total stewardship and parish development.

27. _____ You have adequate office space and the necessary "tools of the trade" for the parish development office.

Computer and printer

Exceptionally efficient and effective software (Microsoft Office,
   Database software [PDS, Parish Soft, etc.])

Telephone and fax line(s)

Website with parish development information

Filing space and cabinets

Access to good copy machine

A budget

Space to meet one-on-one with parishioners and others

Good location of the office in the parish

28. _____ You have looked for ways to collaborate with other Catholic parishes in your area.

29. _____ You have ways of "pipelining" to your parish families at least once a year to determine their attitudes, wants, and needs.

30. _____ Your development personnel (paid and/or volunteer) are members of one or more professional total stewardship and/or development organizations:

A local collaborative group in your area

International stewardship council

NCDC (National Catholic Development Conference)

31. _____ You meaningfully involve between 50–100 people in your development effort on an annual basis through some of the following means:

Input sessions   *Town hall meetings*

Development advisory board   *Development core team*

Long-range pastoral planning   *Cup-of-coffee meetings*

Surveys and questionnaires   *New parishioner socials*

Pastor's cabinet   *Neighborhood outreach ministry*

Other methods

32. _____ You clearly understand the percentage of time that you should spend with each area of Catholic Parish Development.

Constituent records   *Communication*

Fund development   *People engagement*

Total stewardship process   *Special events*

33. _____ You know where you want your development effort to go over the next five years.

34. _____ Ministry/commission leaders are invited to hand in wish lists each year to let you know what they need–big and small.

ASSESSMENT AREA #3: INTERNAL COMMUNICATION

35. _____ The parish staff (however big or small) understands that development is a process and they support the efforts.

36. _____ You have in-serviced all key internal publics on the meaning of Catholic Parish Development:

Parish council

School leaders

Parish staff

Finance council

Commission/ministry leaders

Others of your selection

37. _____ There is some kind of regular communication to all internal publics in regard to what is happening with the development effort.

38. _____ Parish leaders have been given opportunities to get involved in the development efforts, and some are participating.

39. _____ Parish leaders have been invited to input into the mission statement.

40. _____ Parish leaders are involved in the new parishioner welcome effort.

41. _____ Parish leaders (the messengers) clearly understand the mission (the message) of your Catholic parish and speak about it in a positive manner.

42. _____ Your parish leaders understand the parish's history, heritage, and unique qualities.

ASSESSMENT AREA #4:
PROJECTING YOUR PARISH IMAGE AND "BRAND"

43. _____ You have spent a great deal of time and have created an effective, interactive website that can be used for multiple purposes–facts about the parish, registration of new parishioners, online giving, spiritual growth opportunities, etc.

44. _____ The person who answers the phone at your parish is polite and cordial and treats the caller with utmost courtesy.

45. _____ Receptionists have been trained on how to answer the phone at your parish and what to say and not to say.

46. _____ Your parish sends in news articles to the Catholic newspaper and area newspapers on a regular basis about your parish activities.

47. _____ Visitors are welcomed with politeness when they enter the parish office.

48. _____ The bulletin boards within the parish and church and school (if applicable) are decorated with positive messages that reflect the mission.

49. _____ Parishioner concerns are met with immediate attention and concern.

50. _____ The pastor projects a positive image–one that shows a person who has time for others.

51. _____ Parish leaders and volunteers are recognized and affirmed.

52. _____ Your parish participates in diocesan total stewardship and development workshops and uses this time to network.

53. _____ The grounds are clean, the grass is cut, and your parish projects a clean-cut image.

54. _____ There is parking available for all.

55. _____ Parish leaders understand the value of projecting a clean and positive image as any person drives onto or walks around your parish campus.

56. _____ Staff members and parish leaders reflect a professional image by the way they dress, speak, and appear.

ASSESSMENT AREA #5:
PUBLICATIONS/COMMUNICATIONS

57. _____ Your parish has a clear logo or visual image that is recognized and accepted by all.

58. _____ There is one person that "clears" all publications leaving the parish.

59. _____ You have identified those 1–15 words that clearly describe your parish and what you are all about.

60. _____ The image your publications are projecting is the type of image you want to project.

61. _____ You have involved professional expertise to help with your publications and communications.

62. _____ You have created excellent new parishioner materials that you use to welcome new families.

63. _____ You have many methods and events in place for parishioners of all ages to come to your parish and participate in activities and enjoy being on the parish grounds.

64. _____ You have set up an effective e-mail system of communication.

65. _____ You have been able to communicate that your parish has unique qualities and is here to stay.

66. _____ You are putting a formal communication process in place:

Pocket folder   Profile sheet

Newsletter with pictures   Annual report

Parish video   New parishioner welcome brochure

67. _____ You have an annual report in place that lets people know what is done with the money they have invested in your Catholic parish.

68. _____ You are working on a case statement for your parish that clearly shows where the parish has come from, where it is, where it is going, and the many ways people can invest in the parish's future.

69. _____ Your parish takes advantage of using social media outlets to promote and inform.

70. _____ You have a parish newsletter in place.

ASSESSMENT AREA #6: NEW PARISHIONER WELCOME

71. _____ The new parishioner welcome process is well organized and is being effectively implemented.

72. _____ You know what your parishioners really want from their parish–what needs they have.

73. _____ You know how you can address those needs.

74. _____ The entire parish is in constant "welcoming mode."

75. _____ You understand the demographics and economics of your parish boundaries and beyond.

76. _____ With new parishioners, you make sure you capture not only pertinent information but information regarding their e-mail, cell phone number, gifts, talents, areas of expertise and wisdom, etc.

77. _____ Your welcoming effort is evaluated–objectively–at least every two years.

78. _____ You have a ministry or program in place to welcome visitors to your parish.

79. _____ On a regular basis, you personally contact new parish families after they have been in the parish for 6 months to see how they are doing.

ASSESSMENT AREA #7: PARISHIONER INPUT

80. _____ You have an updated database of names, addresses, e-mails, phone numbers, fax numbers, cell phones, etc.

81. _____ Your parishioner base has been receiving good communication from you on a regular basis–and not just the parish bulletin.

82. _____ You host input sessions once or twice per year to seek information from your parish families.

83. _____ You have conducted a parish census sometime within the past five years.

84. _____ You have a neighborhood outreach system in place where the parish is divided into geographical areas and you are able to know who is in each area.

85. _____ You have a core team in place that oversees and provides input into development activities.

86. _____ You host town hall meetings once or twice per year to seek input.

87. _____ You conduct some type of survey or questionnaire once or twice a year to seek input.

ASSESSMENT AREA #8: PARISH STEWARDS

88. _____ You have parishioners who are willing to work with your parish's ministries, organizations, and programs.

89. _____ You have people in your parish who are "movers and shakers."

90. _____ Your volunteers are thanked on a regular basis.

ASSESSMENT AREA #9: TOTAL STEWARDSHIP EDUCATION

91. _____ You have set up a year-round total stewardship education plan that reaches your parish families on a monthly basis.

92. _____ You are educating your parish families to understand the powerful nature of total stewardship of prayer, ministry (time and talent), and offering.

93. _____ Monthly, your parish families are given or e-mailed something to read about total stewardship—with most of the education having very little to do with money.

94. _____ You have educated your parishioners on the close relationship between total stewardship and development.

ASSESSMENT AREA #10: STEWARDSHIP OF PRAYER

95. _____ You offer stewardship of prayer as a key component of total stewardship outreach.

96. _____ Your stewardship of prayer component invites all members of the family to participate, including children.

97. _____ Your stewardship of prayer component invites parishioners to fill out an "intention card" stating what their prayer intentions are and then to offer that intention card in the collection basket on a given Sunday.

98. ____ Your parish takes several weeks to introduce and educate parishioners on stewardship of prayer.

99. ____ You realize that any component of total stewardship must be introduced as personally as possible, not just through direct mail.

100. ____ With stewardship of prayer, you have built in ways to remind parishioners of the prayer commitment.

101. ____ With those parishioners who do not return their prayer intention card, you have built in a follow-up system encouraging them to do so.

102. ____ Stewardship of prayer leads off the total stewardship effort each year.

103. ____ You introduce stewardship of prayer through various media:

Educational literature	*From the pulpit*
Website	*Direct mail*
Phone outreach	*Small faith communities*
Small-group educational sessions	

104. ____ The number of participants in stewardship of prayer keeps increasing by 10% each year.

105. ____ You explain to new parishioners the entire total stewardship effort when they register and are welcomed into the parish.

ASSESSMENT AREA #11:
STEWARDSHIP OF MINISTRY

106. ____ You have identified the main ministries in the parish that you wish to "promote."

107. ____ You host a ministry fair of some kind each year.

108. ____ Your database captures the many gifts, talents, levels of expertise, etc. about each parishioner.

109. _____ You have created a ministry booklet that is distributed to all parish families each year.

110. _____ Stewardship of ministry is formally introduced each year and is defined not only as time and talent but also as wisdom, expertise, and community resources.

ASSESSMENT AREA #12: STEWARDSHIP OF OFFERING

111. _____ Your stewardship of offering is seen as part of the entire package of total stewardship.

112. _____ "Stewardship Sunday" in your parish is not defined as a weekend to just collect money.

113. _____ Because of the strong education component offered throughout the year, your total stewardship effort is seen as inviting gifts of prayer, ministry, and offering.

114. _____ With stewardship of offering, you have built a comprehensive distribution and follow-up system that is centered as much around personal outreach as possible.

115. _____ During the stewardship of offering phase of your total stewardship process, you also remind people of their gifts of prayer and ministry.

116. _____ You offer a weekly and/or monthly payment breakdown sheet so parishioners can see what a $15/week financial contribution would mean over a 12-month period of time.

117. _____ You spend time educating parishioners on the differences between stewardship of offering, special collections, sacrificial giving, and tithing.

118. _____ Your overall approach in stewardship of offering is toward promoting participation.

119. _____ Although 100% participation from all parish families may be unrealistic, you strive for over 75% participation of your parish families in stewardship of offering.

120. _____ On the front end of introducing stewardship of offering, a member of the finance council gives a financial report stating how parish leaders have been excellent stewards of the money that has been entrusted to them.

121. _____ You provide the parish with some kind of report that explains and shows what is done with the money that is given to the parish.

ASSESSMENT AREA #13: ENDOWMENT

122. _____ You have begun to build an endowment fund for your parish.

123. _____ Your endowment effort is set up so the corpus of that fund is never touched.

124. _____ Your endowment growth is through major gifts and/or your planned giving efforts.

125. _____ Your parish leadership is actually making a commitment to building the endowment and not just paying "lip service" to it.

ASSESSMENT AREA #14: MEMORIAL GIFTS

126. _____ You have a formal memorial gift program in place for your parish.

127. _____ You have literature that explains the many opportunities for people to make a memorial gift through the parish.

ASSESSMENT AREA #15: CAPITAL CAMPAIGN

128. _____ Your parish leaders recognize the value of conducting a capital campaign every 8–10 years in order to construct new facilities, renovate and/or restore existing ones, retire debt, and/or build endowment.

129. _____ Your parish leaders understand how the capital campaign fits into the overall development effort.

ASSESSMENT AREA #16: PLANNED GIVING

130. _____ You have a basic understanding of planned giving and realize that this is an area that is a very important component of your development effort.

131. _____ You are using your newsletter to explain planned giving opportunities.

132. _____ You have considered offering educational sessions at some time in the future.

133. _____ You have identified those people in your parish who have expertise in planned giving.

134. _____ Your parish has a tax attorney who can advise the parish and donors of the many options of a planned/deferred giving program.

135. _____ Your parish has identified those potential donors who may have an interest in planned giving.

136. _____ Your development "officers" have received the necessary training in order to understand planned giving.

137. _____ Your parish has gathered the important planned-giving literature that is available in order to form a library of materials.

ASSESSMENT AREA #17: THE MAGIC OF CREATIVITY

138. _____ Your parish leaders are willing to listen to new ideas, new concepts, and new dreams–and then act on them.

139. _____ Your parish leaders do not walk around with the attitude that they have all the answers.

140. _____ Your parish leaders are not threatened by "new" people and the positive impact that they could have on your parish.

141. _____ You realize that a visionary long-range, pastoral plan can be created only by leaders with vision.

142. _____ Your parish has taken a strong stand *against* the following statement: "But we've always done it that way."

143. _____ Everyone understands the statement: "If you always approach a problem or situation the same way, you'll always end up in the same place."

144. _____ Your parish leaders are willing to listen to new ideas and new concepts and then get excited and involved in them.

145. _____ Your development efforts are always seeking new ways to improve.

HOW TO SCORE
Give yourself 2 points for every TRUE answer; 1 point for every SOMEWHAT answer and 0 points for every FALSE answer.

YOUR TOTAL SCORE: _____

250–290: Outstanding! You have a great Catholic Parish Development effort that is involving people, creating new resource opportunities, and building a strong future—all with the right components. Keep moving forward.

210–249: Very Good. You certainly have a fine effort in place and are headed in the right direction for the future. Take a strong look at those statements where you checked either FALSE or SOMEWHAT. Those are the areas you need to assess for future growth.

170–209: Good. Your parish has put some key elements in place. Go back and look at those statements where you checked either FALSE or SOMEWHAT. Those are the areas that you need to assess and improve in order to build a solid foundation for the future.

120–169: Need Some Work. Don't get discouraged. It may be that you are just beginning and your effort is just getting off the ground. If so, concentrate on assessment areas #1–7 when you begin. Building the right foundation is half the battle. Try to rest a little easier, knowing that beginning Catholic Parish Development the right way will keep you from spinning your wheels down the road.

1–119: A Real Challenge. Please refer to the above comments under "Need Some Work." Also, ask yourself this question: Did I give myself enough credit on the TFS Test?

Lesson Nine: Seek Input from Parishioners

|| "We need to make our own the ancient pastoral
|| wisdom which encouraged pastors to listen more
|| widely to the entire People of God." SAINT JOHN PAUL II

In implementing a vibrant Catholic development effort, it is always important to test the pulse of the parish at least once per year—usually with a parish-wide survey. Obviously, there are other methods of inviting input, all the way from input sessions to questionnaires to interviews to town hall meetings, etc. Let's look at three ways that we have found to be effective.

I. SAMPLE PARISH SURVEY

A simple, written survey allows parish leaders to understand what parishioners are feeling; if created properly, the instrument can provide excellent data and information about your parish families. This survey can be taken both online as well as in the pew. In working with your core team, it will be important to note the major areas where further feedback would be beneficial. Listed below is a *sample* survey we have used with a number of parishes—with some guidance as to how to distribute it. The specific areas of the survey usually come from discussions with parish leaders and the core team. We strongly recommend that you format the survey so that it fits on *one* sheet of paper—front and back.

SAMPLE PARISH SURVEY

Directions: *As part of the parish development process now in place at _____, the core team is conducting a parish-wide survey designed to identify present and future needs in a number of areas. Your participation will greatly assist us in determining what is best for the parish. Please take a few minutes to complete the following survey. It will be most beneficial.*

Please circle: Parishioner   Guest

Please circle your age: 18-25   26-35   36-50   51-65   Over 65

If a parishioner, how long have you been a member of the parish?
_____ years

Children now in _____ Catholic School?   ☐ Yes ☐ No

Children now in Religious Education Program?   ☐ Yes ☐ No

Please circle the number that most closely matches your opinion:

1. Our celebration of liturgy meets my needs as a Roman Catholic.

Strongly agree		Agree		Neutral		Disagree		Strongly disagree		No Answer
10	9	8	7	6	5	4	3	2	1	NA

2. Parish and school leaders do an excellent job of communicating with me regarding activities, ministries, calendar events, and pertinent topics.

Strongly agree		Agree		Neutral		Disagree		Strongly disagree		No Answer
10	9	8	7	6	5	4	3	2	1	NA

3. There are many opportunities for me to spiritually grow at _____ Parish.

Strongly agree		Agree		Neutral		Disagree		Strongly disagree		No Answer
10	9	8	7	6	5	4	3	2	1	NA

4. There are many opportunities for our youth to become involved at _____ Parish.

Strongly agree		Agree		Neutral		Disagree		Strongly disagree		No Answer
10	9	8	7	6	5	4	3	2	1	NA

5. _____ Parish is a warm, welcoming parish that reaches out to all families.

Strongly agree		Agree		Neutral		Disagree		Strongly disagree		No Answer
10	9	8	7	6	5	4	3	2	1	NA

6. The parish successfully meets my family's religious education needs.

Strongly agree		Agree		Neutral		Disagree		Strongly disagree		No Answer
10	9	8	7	6	5	4	3	2	1	NA

7. The buildings and grounds of our parish are adequate and meet the needs of our ministries.

Strongly agree		Agree		Neutral		Disagree		Strongly disagree		No Answer
10	9	8	7	6	5	4	3	2	1	NA

Any further comments?

If you would like to know the results of the survey or would like further information, please complete the following:

Name _____

Address _____

City _____ Zip _____ Phone _____

E-mail address _____

SURVEY INSTRUCTIONS FOR THOSE CONDUCTING THE IN-PEW SURVEY

- Surveys should be conducted at each Mass on Saturday and Sunday.
- Surveys should be filled in and picked up at each Mass.
- Please use different colored surveys for each Mass.
- One way to distribute the survey is for core team members to put the surveys and pencils in the pews *before* each Mass. Place the surveys approximately every three feet in the pews.
- Using a recent Mass census (count), it is a good idea to count out stacks of surveys for each Mass beforehand.
- Before or after the homily, the celebrant or a core team member should give directions to everyone on how to fill in the survey. Also, we have found that if the celebrant or core team member slowly reads the survey out loud, 90% of the people will fill it in as he or she reads.
- Parishioners should leave the surveys and the pencils in the pews after Mass, and the core team members pick them up. OR, when parishioners finish filling in the survey, they can simply fold the survey and pass it to the center aisle to be picked up by the ushers.
- People standing in the back of church and along the side walls should be handed a survey and pencil by a core team member. Core team members should also offer to pick up the surveys from these people after the presentation.
- For confidentiality sake, people are welcome to fold the survey in half if that makes them feel more comfortable.
- At the end of each Mass, core team members should pick up the surveys and pencils from the pews.
- Surveys should be filled in individually and not by a couple. The preferred age to fill in a survey is 16 years old and above.
- Parishioners are welcome to stay in church and finish the survey after Mass is over. Please discourage them from taking the survey home.

Please remember that this survey can also be created with Survey Monkey, and it can be e-mailed (with the link) to each parish family, noting in the e-mail: "If you filled in this survey at any of the Masses this past weekend, it is not necessary to fill it in again."

2. INPUT SESSIONS AND THEIR VALUE

Definition We define an input session as a meeting of approximately 10–15 people who are randomly invited to attend a 50-minute session and focus on 3–4 questions for discussion. The input session is usually facilitated by a core team member, and there is a clear agenda.

Rationale As part of the 7-"I" process of parish development, the input session fits into the Invite stage. (Please refer to the 7-"I" philosophy in Lesson One). This is an excellent way to invite people and get them interested in what is going on in your parish. It can be the beginning of your relationship with them—whether they are involved or uninvolved; it is important for you to get to know them and vice versa. Input sessions provide that introduction and invitation.

When done correctly, we find them to be very successful because:
- People are personally invited;
- The person inviting them is the pastor;
- You are giving people a choice of times and dates;
- People really enjoy giving their opinion;
- A personal phone call is the follow-up;
- They know they are not being asked to serve on a committee that meets all the time;
- They know they are being asked to attend a session that lasts for only one hour at the most;
- There is an established agenda.

Through the years, we have found that input sessions allow you to identify many of the future leaders of your parish community. It is an excellent way to begin the relationship.

The Process

1. Randomly select the people you wish to invite from a list of parishioners.

2. Plan to conduct two nights of input sessions with three sessions per night (6:00 PM; 7:00 PM; 8:00 PM). You will want to have approximately 10–15 people in each session.

3. You want to invite twice as many people as you expect will come. If you get more, that is great.

4. For example, with a list of 540 parish families, and you have scheduled two nights of input sessions—or six sessions—you should invite 180 people, or every third name on the list. Please keep in mind that some people will feel left out. That is OK as long as you let them know that you will be conducting another series in the future.

5. Mail out letters. (E-mailed invitations are not as effective. Remember: you are dealing with all different age groups.)
   - The letter can be modeled on the sample letter on page 83.
   - Personally address—no mailing label—and sign the letters.
   - Use a first-class stamp.

6. Within one week, there should be the follow-up phone call from a core team member. There is a great opportunity for public relations here, so make sure you've got someone who is wonderful on the phone. Sample conversation:

   "Hi. Mary, this is Betty, and I am calling on behalf of (*name of parish*). Mary, did you receive the letter from Father _____ inviting you to one of the input sessions that we will be having here at the parish next week? You did? Great. Mary, which one of those six sessions will be most convenient for you to attend?

7. When people arrive, greeters show them where to park and show them where to go for the session. Have signs posted that direct people to the meeting space.

8. You should have the following:
- An agenda with the following points:
  Opening Prayer
  Welcome
  Introductions
  Purpose of the input session
  Guidelines
  Three questions
  Wrap-up
  Individual input sheet
- An individual input sheet
- Name tags
- Refreshments
- The pastor and/or parish leaders thanking people personally for coming

9. At five minutes to the hour, people are invited into the room—please see next section.

10. Input session is conducted. The three questions that work the best are:
- What do you see as the present strengths (working well) of the parish?
- What are the greatest needs (improvements) that currently exist in the parish?
- As we look to the future, what would you like to see here (vision) at (*name of parish*)? (programs, ministries, buildings, renovations, etc.)

11. Within 2–3 weeks of the input session, an input session report, listing the highlights, is mailed to all people who attended. This report summarizes all of the sessions.

12. A thank-you letter is sent with the report.

Input Session Procedure and Guidelines

1. The room should be arranged in a circle or semi-circle so people can see each other.

2. The facilitator(s) needs to be at the focal point of the room.

3. There should be a scribe that the parish/facilitator(s) appoints.
   - No tape/video recorders

4. The pastor or some other "parish official" thanks people for attending, opens with a prayer, and then leaves the room.

5. Process is handed over to a facilitator(s)—usually a core team member(s).

6. Facilitator follows this process:
   - Introduces himself/herself;
   - Has each person introduce himself/herself and state relationship with the parish;
   - Goes over the guidelines;
   - Introduces the first question and opens up the discussion;
   - Keeps track of time every step of the way;
   - At ten minutes to the hour, the facilitator wraps up the session and has people walking out by five minutes to the hour.

7. Written guidelines should be on the agenda, distributed at the beginning of the session, along with the individual input sheet. Here are the guidelines.
   - We would like to hear from everyone.
   - Everyone is on equal ground.
   - If there is anything that you would like to bring forth but do not want to discuss it, please use the individual input sheet to write your thoughts. *Everyone* will be asked to hand in their input sheet at the end of the session.
   - We are not here to discuss personalities.
   - Please: no responses or rebuttals to comments made.

- We are not here to argue.
- We will be finished in 50-55 minutes.
- You will receive a written report within two to four weeks.

8. Questions that are helpful to keep the small group moving along:
- What do you think?
- Could you be more specific?
- What else?
- What are your concerns?
- How do you feel about that?
- What solutions are available to us?
- Could you clarify your position/point for us?
- Why do you feel that way?

9. The facilitator and the scribe should pay close attention to those people who raise key issues and seem to want to get more involved in the future. The scribe should write down their names. That is why "big" name tags are essential.

The Written Report
The written report is done after all the sessions and usually follows this outline:
- Purpose of the input sessions
- Times and places
- Questions asked
- Key issues raised
- Major "threads" that could be woven throughout all the sessions
- Future focus

This report is usually 2–3 pages in length and should not get into a lot of real controversial "stuff." That should be handled on an individual basis or addressed separately. The written report should summarize the sessions and highlight the answers to the three questions. No individual names should ever be mentioned in the report.

Sample Letter of Invite to an Input Session

Date

Dear _____ ,

I am writing to invite you to a 50–55-minute input session for (name of parish). As parish leaders continue to seek ways to improve how we listen to our parish families, we believe it is important to gather further input and opinion regarding the future of the parish. Over the next 12 months, we will be inviting many people throughout our parish who will assume an active role in determining our immediate direction and future focus.

We will be conducting input sessions at 6:00 PM, 7:00 PM, and 8:00 PM on two different dates at (location). Those dates are: _____ . We would greatly appreciate it if you could attend one of these six sessions. We will be calling you within the next week to see which time is best for you.

The three questions we will be asking are:

- What do you see as the present strengths (working well) of the parish?
- What are the greatest needs (improvements) that currently exist in the parish?
- As we look to the future, what would you like to see here (vision) at (name of parish)? (programs, ministries, buildings, renovations, etc.)

Thank you for your consideration, and we hope to see you at one of these opportunities for input and discussion.

Sincerely,
(Pastor)

Note to the Reader

Input sessions continue to be a wonderful way to invite and involve people into the life of a parish. Please keep in mind that attendance will vary; however, remember that you are inviting many people whom you do not know at all. These are second- and third-ripple people. And it does take time to engage them, so don't get discouraged.

3. THE ULTIMATE QUESTION SURVEY

The Ultimate Question is not a new book on theology. The book's author is Fred Reichheld. Harvard Business Press published the book in 2006. It has a broad application to just about any organization, including Catholic parishes. One of the main outcomes of this survey is getting the parish's Net Promoter Score, or NPS. This is based on the fundamental perspective that parishioners in a Catholic parish can be divided into three categories: *Promoters*, *Passives*, and *Detractors*.

By asking one simple question—How likely is it that you would recommend (your Catholic parish) to a friend, neighbor, or family member?—you can get a clear measure of your parish's performance through your parishioner's eyes. Parishioners respond on a 10-point scale and are categorized as follows:

Promoters (*score 9–10*) are loyal enthusiasts who will keep "promoting" and referring the parish to others, thereby fueling growth.

Passives (*score 7–8*) are satisfied but unenthusiastic parishioners who are vulnerable to competitive offerings.

Detractors (*score 0–6*) are unhappy parishioners who can damage your image and impede growth through negative word-of-mouth.

To calculate your parish's NPS, you would take the percentage of people who took the survey who are Promoters and subtract the percentage from those who are Detractors.

NPS = % of Promoters (9s and 10s) − % of Detractors (0–6)

NOTE

Passives are not counted into the formula.

There is also a Part B to the question. After circling a number 0–10, the person filling in the survey is then asked to respond to Part B. "If you did not give us a score of 10, please explain what we need to do and/or address so that the next time you take this survey, the score you give us will either be a 10 or close to it." Obviously, this provides some excellent qualitative data that can then be categorized and used in numerous ways.

We recommend that a parish should ask The Ultimate Question at least once a year. In our work with parishes, we find that the following NPS percentages represent what is acceptable and what is not.

Outstanding: Above 65%
Average: 50%–64%
Below Average: 35%–49%
Dismal: Below 34%

The easy part about The Ultimate Question survey is that it can be conducted online by sending an e-mail to every parish family with the link to the survey.

As we said, in building your parish *development* efforts around the 7 "I"s (*identify, inform, invite, involve, implement, invest,* and *improve*) and consistently seeking input from your constituents, this plugs in to the most important "I" of them all: *invite.* Through in-pew surveys, input sessions, and The Ultimate Question, parishes can personally invite people to belong.

Questions, Exercises, and Next Best Steps for Lesson Nine

1. What is your parish's position and philosophy on seeking input on a consistent basis from all parish families? Please explain.

2. Does your parish seek input (surveys, questionnaires, etc.) from your constituents on an annual basis? If so, how is this done?

3. What type of input instrument(s) did you use to seek the input?

4. Was the input valuable? If so, in what ways were you able to use the results in order to continually improve?

5. If you do seek input on a regular basis, have you communicated the survey results to the community? If so, how did you do this and what kind of feedback did you receive?

6. In terms of seeking input from your parish families, please check YES or NO if you have sought input (interviews, surveys, input sessions, questionnaires, etc.) from any of the following groups within the past 12 months:

Parish staff	☐ Yes	☐ No
Parish council	☐ Yes	☐ No
Finance council	☐ Yes	☐ No
Ministry leaders	☐ Yes	☐ No
School staff (if applicable)	☐ Yes	☐ No
Parishioners	☐ Yes	☐ No
Neighbors	☐ Yes	☐ No

7. Based on the above question, please highlight which of the above group(s) you believe would be the most important to seek input from within the next 12 months.

8. In this lesson, we refer to three main instruments in order to seek input. One is to conduct input sessions; that process is explained in detail in this lesson. The other is to conduct the parish survey, which can be conducted with hard copies at each Mass as well as online. And the third way is to conduct The Ultimate Question survey. Survey Monkey is an excellent (and inexpensive) way to do the latter one online. Based on the groups in #6 where you checked YES, please seek their input by using the parish survey and/or conducting input sessions and/or conducting The Ultimate Question. Please do this within the next 6 months.

Lesson Ten: Create and/or Affirm the Parish Mission/ Vision for the Future

|| **"Vision gives us courage to speak when we might want to remain silent."** ACTS 18:9

In the Spirituality Series, Henri J.M. Nouwen talks about *A Spirituality of Fundraising*. For so many years, we have stayed away from using the word *fund-raising* to equally define Catholic development; however, in *A Spirituality of Fundraising*, Nouwen elevates the word into a much wider view and clearly articulates what we have always believed. He speaks of *fund-raising* in the same light as *development*. As he says, development is not a response to a crisis, even though that may be the starting point for some Catholic parishes who decide they need to hire a development director or put on a fund-raiser. Development is a ministry.

To quote from Nouwen, "[Development] is, first and foremost, a form of ministry. It is a way of announcing our vision and inviting other people into our mission. Vision and mission are so central to the life of God's people that without vision we perish and without mission we lose our way (Prov 29:18; 2 Kings 21:1–9). Vision brings together needs and resources to meet those needs (Acts 9:1–19). Vision also shows us new directions and opportunities for our mission (Acts 16:9–10)."

The reason why we say that Nouwen's view is much wider than how many define *fund-raising* can be seen in this next passage. "When we seek to raise funds we are not saying, 'Please could you help us out because lately it's been hard.' Rather, we are declaring, 'We have a vision that is amazing and exciting. We are inviting you to invest yourself through the resources that God has given you—your energy, your prayers, and your money—in this work to which God has called us.' Our invitation is clear and confident because we trust that our vision and mission are like 'trees planted by streams of water, which yield their fruit in its season, and their leaves do not wither' (Ps 1:3)."

Being able to clearly articulate the mission and vision of your parish is so important, and it becomes powerful when the leaders of the parish all share the same message. When you are able to do that, then there should be no hesitancy in inviting people to invest their resources (talents, wisdom, finances, prayer, etc.) in your parish. After all, as we have said for many years, development is all about inviting people to share the resources that God has given us; and through that sharing we are able to develop and advance our mission and vision.

Perhaps it is time to revisit your mission and vision statements and see if they are relevant, compelling, and exciting. Maybe it is time to pour new wine into new wineskins, for, as Nouwen says, "Vision gives us courage to speak when we might want to otherwise remain silent."

For those parishes that have not revisited their mission/vision statements or who are in need of creating/revising, we suggest that you successfully complete the following statements:

- We are the people who...
- We provide...
- We want to be seen as...

The words and phrases that you use in completing these statements will lead you to your mission and vision language. An example of a large parish who went through this process is the National Shrine of the Little Flower Basilica in the Archdiocese of Detroit. Their mission and vision statements are compelling.

Mission Statement

In the spirit of St. Therese, the National Shrine of the Little Flower Basilica exists to bring everyone in our community to an encounter with Christ, to grow in His love, and to go forth sharing the Good News of Jesus Christ to all. [44 words]

Vision Statement

The National Shrine of the Little Flower Basilica will be a band of joyful missionary disciples who go forth filled with the love of Christ, in the spirit of St. Therese, giving witness to the Good News, sharing the faith through word and action, thus drawing all to communion in Christ. [51 words]

So what is your constant purpose (mission)? What drives the day-to-day thinking and decision-making in your parish? What are those words and phrases that clearly define what your parish is all about and how you operate and build your faith community on a consistent basis? In addition, where is your parish going and what is it striving to be (vision)? What will excite people to join your parish, and what will compel people to want to get involved? What is your "WOW"? These are all questions that parish leaders need to discuss and be able to answer—throughout all forms and means of communication.

Questions, Exercises, and Next Best Steps for Lesson Ten

With the above in mind, here are some questions we invite you to consider:

1. Is your parish mission statement clear and compelling (and short), and does it state the constant purpose of what you do day to day? Please explain.

2. Does your parish have a vision that can be clearly articulated in the spoken and written word that shows the dynamic direction your parish is headed? Please explain.

3. Do your mission and vision create a compelling case for why people should want to get involved with your parish? Please explain.

4. Do all of your key messengers (pastor, staff, councils, ministry leaders, etc.) share the same vision and mission (messages)? Please explain.

5. Are these messages collectively agreed upon by all of the messengers? (In other words, is there a unified effort by all messengers to create and share your mission and vision?) Please explain.

6. Is your vision unique, distinctive, and exciting to share? Please explain.

7. Are these messages displayed throughout the parish and woven into all of your communication vehicles? Please explain.

Lesson Eleven: Create the Strategic Plan for Parish Development

|| "The future starts today, not tomorrow."
|| SAINT JOHN PAUL II

PHILOSOPHY AND RATIONALE

As we have suggested throughout the book, in order for Catholic Parish Development (CPD) to come alive, there needs to be a plan of action—a roadmap for the parish to follow in order to be successful in accomplishing the ultimate goal, bringing people to Christ and Christ to people.

When the Institute for School and Parish Development (ISPD) began in 1989, we realized four key themes needed to be articulated in order for this kind of planning to flourish.

- The first was that we needed to have people understand that the parish mission and vision need to be the foundation for everything a parish does.
- Second, we needed to have people understand that Catholic Parish Development is a series of processes that come together to form a unique system that helps a parish advance and grow. And, by development—as we have said—we do not mean money; we mean how a parish develops over time.
- Third, creating a strategic plan for Catholic Parish Development is *not* the same thing as creating a strategic plan for the entire parish. This CPD strategic plan focuses on the six main areas of parish development:
  - » Constituent records,
  - » Parish communication,
  - » People engagement,
  - » Fund development,
  - » Total stewardship process,
  - » Special events.

This is not planning that deals with facilities or music ministry or liturgy or religious education; this is planning that focuses on developing the resources of the parish by making sure all of the six above areas are active and being implemented.

- Fourth, we needed to define development as the meaningful involvement of people in that parish's mission and vision for the future. *Belonging leads to believing.*

When we now talk about creating the strategic plan for parish development, ISPD's philosophy takes the front seat. Using the numbers from Gallup, how do we affirm the 30% already involved, and how do we reach the 30% uninvolved and the 40% actively disengaged? In this age of the New Evangelization, the essential role of the layperson has been emphasized as never before, and that leads us to one of the greatest challenges we face in developing our parishes: How do we create the roadways, avenues, and vehicles to invite and involve and engage people into the life of the church?

There are many ways to approach strategic planning like this. Back when I was a Catholic school administrator, I used to call in three to four people (teacher, board member, and alum), and we wrote the mission statement and created a plan of action. Quick. Easy. Not time consuming at all. We were "in and out" in two sessions. However, there was no buy-in; there was no ownership; others did not see this as their plan. We did not engage people and take full advantage of their many gifts. I remember one person on the board (who was president of his own company) telling me, "You're in charge; you set the tone; you set the vision; you set everything, and people need to fall in line and follow." That did not prove to be successful in a Catholic school and is even less successful in a Catholic parish, even though there are those today who still believe that letting the pastor and the parish council create the plan of action is the best way to handle things. We believe there is a better way, one that can involve more people.

Today, strategic planning (of any kind) in a Catholic parish can be exciting, invigorating, and serve as a wonderful way to engage people and call them to action. It needs to be realistic and reasonable, yet challenging and courageous, while affirming and inspiring. With this thought and good understanding of the previous lessons, we view and approach Catholic Parish Development planning as a wonderful opportunity to put together a series of steps and processes that will reach out beyond the first ripple of people, who always raise their hand, and invite many others to step forward and gain a clearer understanding of their role and value in the church. This is outlined and explained in this lesson.

I. INFRASTRUCTURE STEPS
Executive Committee
When a parish begins to work on its strategic plan for development, it is important to establish the "go to" people. You need to communicate with, and rely upon the wisdom and expertise of, a handful of people—usually the pastor, a member of the parish staff, one or two members from the parish council, a member of the parish development core team (if applicable), a member of the finance council, and a representative from the Catholic school—if there is one. We call this the executive committee, and they usually meet twice per month or more often, if needed. The executive committee signs off on and makes decisions on some key initiatives that need to be made in regards to the process—the people to invite to be part of the core team (if there is not already one in place), the place and time of the meetings in the strategic planning process, the finalization of the communication pieces in the process, the final list of challenges, etc.

Core Team
This is the team we spoke of in Lesson Seven; this is the group of 15–20 dedicated and committed people who create, implement, and sustain the processes. The initial thrust is toward three areas:

Education: educate individuals and groups within the parish about the process and what is being done;

Facilitation: facilitate the small-group work in the planning process;

Implementation: implement the various strategies and steps of the planning process as we move through the various stages from month to month.

II. PARISH SURVEY AND ASSESSMENT

Once the executive committee and the core team are in place, it will be important to assess the parish and gather both qualitative as well as quantitative data. In Lesson Nine, we talked about three ways to receive parish input: input sessions, parish survey, and The Ultimate Question. Using one of these input vehicles on the front end of this strategic planning process will give you excellent information on how parishioners view the parish, what areas they will affirm, and what areas need improvement. I particularly like The Ultimate Question or some variation of it, simply because this can all be done online (e.g., Survey Monkey). You can reach people who do not sit in the pews every weekend, simply because you are sending out e-mail invitations to everyone and promoting the survey every chance you can, especially by providing the link for people to go fill it out. In addition, it greatly helps if you can launch a phone outreach to every parish family, encouraging them to fill in the online survey.

In addition, the core team can have 1–2 meetings where the following question can be answered—both verbally and in the written word: *In regards to Catholic Parish Development and stewardship in our parish, what do you believe to be the present strengths, the present weaknesses, the future opportunities, and the future threats to advancing our parish in the future?* This SWOT analysis can provoke wonderful discussion and also provide a basis for identifying the challenges the parish faces in this strategic planning process. Please remember that you are doing a SWOT on parish development (resources).

III. FOUNDATIONAL STEPS IN THE PROCESS

Mission and Vision Statement(s) In the beginning of this process, it will be important to *anchor* the thinking and forward movement with the parish mission and vision statement(s). I would not move forward if this is not in place. The previous lesson delved into this subject.

Prayer for the Process At the beginning of the process, we encourage the parish to create a prayer in order to pray for the success of the planning process. The prayer is used at every meeting and every gathering.

Some parishes seek out prayer groups within the parish to regularly and consistently say the prayer that has been created for the planning process.

Communication: The Executive Committee and the Core Team The executive committee should debrief after each core team and parish planning team meeting.

Communication: Announcement of the Process The planning process is usually introduced to the parish in four ways:
- The pastor will either write something in the bulletin announcing that the parish is entering into a planning process in order to create a strategic plan for parish development and/or he will announce the process from the pulpit;
- There will be a bulletin insert on a given weekend when the process is announced and explained;
- Core team members will be assigned to go out to the key ministries of the parish (who meet on a regular and consistent basis) and get on their agenda for 5–10 minutes to explain the process (see below);
- The copy points in the bulletin insert are also put on the website, and many parishes have actually created a special section (or button) on their website where updates and

schedules and recaps can be placed as the planning process moves along.

Communication: Outreach to Ministries Usually by the second core team meeting, core team members have been asked to sign up to be the connection to one or two ministries that the executive committee believes would be good to communicate with. These are ministries that meet on a regular and consistent basis. The final assignments are usually made in between the second and the third core team meeting. What is important here is that the handout document, which could be called *Parish Development Update*, is ready for distribution. This is a one-page document that the core team member(s) should bring to hand out to the ministries they are visiting. The handout explains the process and should answer most questions. Here are some sample articles for the first issue of the *Parish Development Update*.

Charting a New Course

(Name of parish) will begin to chart a new course for our future. Parish leaders are now focusing on the need to plan on how we can invite, involve, and engage more people in our faith community. During the next 8–10 months, we will be inviting hundreds of people to help us create a strategic plan for development and stewardship.

As we begin this new chapter in our history, the process that we will follow is: in order to create the plans and strategic initiatives for the future development of our parish, we will plan to reach out to our entire community and invite your input and best wisdom. Your recommendations will certainly be considered as we chart a new course for the future.

Beginning with this *Update*, you will be kept informed about various activities, processes, and opportunities geared toward community input and people engagement. There will be many opportunities for everyone to help us create a dynamic new way to engage people.

GETTING STARTED—The process has already begun. We have worked with parish leaders to assess our present situation in a number of areas: governance, involvement of people, stewardship, communication, welcoming, and others.

THE CORE TEAM—We have formed a parish development core team to lead this process for our community. These volunteers represent diverse ministries and interests of our parish family. The core team members have committed themselves to help give their best direction and guidance and will work closely with our pastor and parish staff to facilitate our process. Members of the core team are: (list alphabetically)

PARISH SURVEY—We invite you to fill in a short survey that will give us further information about the needs and areas of improvement in the parish. Please click on the following link: (show link)

As this process unfolds, all parish families will be invited to share your thoughts and ideas through the survey, a planning team, the Parish Convocation, and/or one of the implementation teams when we move to the implementation stage.

Here is the ministry outreach process: Core team members are sent their assignments with the contact information for the ministry or ministries for which they are responsible.

Core team members make contact with the person in charge of

that ministry and schedule a time to meet. "Good morning, this is (name of core team member), and I am a member of the newly formed core team here at (name of parish). Hopefully, you have heard from (name of pastor) who announced recently that the parish is undertaking a strategic planning process focusing on parish development and people engagement. I would like to schedule a time to come and speak with the adult choir (for example) for about 5–10 minutes, give them a handout that explains the process, and then ask if they have any questions. We want to make sure we keep our ministries informed about the process. When would be the best time for us to visit?"

- Core team members go to the ministry gathering, introduce themselves as a member of the core team, and then hand out the document. They can use the handout as notes to let people know about the process, or they can verbally go over the highlights and then refer to the document for more details.
- At the end of the short presentation, core team members should ask if there are any questions. If there are questions they do not have the answer for, they should say, "In visiting the ministries, we are writing down all of the questions, and in each issue of the *Update* we will be answering them. Thank you for asking."
- The core team members should bring back the questions to the next core team meeting, and they should be prepared to give a short 1–3 minute recap of their visit.
- Midway through the process (usually before the last development advisory council meeting) the core team members should revisit the ministries and give them an update and personally invite them to the convocation.

Communication: Throughout the Strategic Planning Process
Throughout the process, a number of communication vehicles should be implemented:
- Monthly or every other month *Update* for bulletin insert;

- E-mail blasts of the *Update* to all parish families;
- Announcements and updates from the pulpit by the pastor and selected core team members;
- Announcements and update via the school communication documents (if applicable);
- Updates on the website;
- Social media updates;
- Visits to the ministries;
- Article(s) about the process in parish communication documents;
- Other suggestions by the core team.

Catholic Parish Development Educational Workshop If possible, it is great to present an educational workshop for three groups of people:
- Core team,
- Ministry leaders,
- Staff members.

This workshop is usually divided into four parts:
- A short explanation about the strategic plan for parish development process;
- A brief summary of the parish survey;
- Education about what Catholic Parish Development really is;
- A call to action.

The purpose of the presentation is to light some new fires, suggest some possible changes, and challenge the parish to be the exceptional parish in this age of the New Evangelization.

IV. CREATING THE CHALLENGES
Through the discussions with core team members, and with the results of the parish-wide survey, you now have assembled a great deal of qualitative information in regard to how people feel about

the parish. If you use The Ultimate Question Survey, Part B asks the question: "If you did not give us a score of 9 or 10, what would we need to do between now and when you would be invited to take the survey again in twelve months that would move your score closer to 10?" There will be all kinds of comments, and many of these provide the basis for the challenges you will need to solve.

Here is a random list of sample Catholic Parish Development challenges that we have seen over the past several years:

1. How can (name of parish) better engage the young people of our parish and serve as a "gateway for involvement" as they move from adolescence into adulthood (i.e., ages 15–30)?

2. How can (name of parish) and (name of parish school) better communicate and collaborate with each other and thereby build a stronger relationship for the future?

3. How can (name of parish) continue to reach out and engage the diverse groups of people (i.e. ethnic, age, socioeconomic) in our parish and thereby build a stronger faith community for all?

4. How can (name of parish) offer more opportunities and at the same time make it easier for young families to become more involved?

5. How can (name of parish) continue to build a strong communication system (both internally and externally), with clear messaging, and in so doing determine the best communication vehicles for the parish?

6. How can (name of parish) better focus on service and mission and thereby make a more positive impact on the surrounding community?

7. How can we better educate all parish families on the importance of total stewardship and the impact of their many gifts to their parish?

8. How can we reach out and personally engage the 30% uninvolved and 40% active disengaged into the life of our parish, including our nontraditional families?

9. How can we increase enrollment in (name of parish school)?

10. How can we improve our overall communication here at (name of parish), especially with those who do not attend Mass on a regular basis?

11. How can we become a more warm, welcoming, and engaging parish?

While these are sample challenges, it is important to understand that, either directly or indirectly, these challenges focus on those six areas of Catholic Parish Development: 1. Constituent records, 2. Communications, 3. Fund development, 4. Total stewardship process, 5. People engagement, 6. Special events.

V. INVITING AND ESTABLISHING THE DEVELOPMENT ADVISORY COUNCIL FOR THREE MEETINGS

The core team, which obviously includes the executive committee, is asked to nominate people for the development advisory council. We encourage each core team member to come up with the names of 10 people who are not that involved in the parish or who may be new to it. And, we like each core team member to suggest the names of 5 people who are already involved. We are trying to get a configuration of 60% "not that much involved" in the parish and 40% "involved."

Once you look at the nominations and pay close attention to the duplicates, triplicates, etc., we encourage you to invite 125–150 people in order to get the 75+ you should have in the planning process.

A personal letter should be sent to each person who is invited, and in that letter please include a copy of the agenda for the first development advisory council (DAC) meeting. Also included in the letter are the dates of the three meetings. The letter should be personally signed by the pastor. The core team should split up the list and make phone calls to personally invite each person. It is also helpful to provide the core team with the entire list of people who are invited; ask them to look at the list; if they see anyone on the list that they know and see all the time, suggest that the core team member—informally—mention that they saw their name on the invitee list and that they would love to have them join the planning process for these three meetings.

Before the first DAC meeting, please make sure that all those who are invited know what the challenges are. This can be done by including them in the agenda for the first DAC meeting. (It is best to limit the number of challenges to 6–8.) Below is a sample letter.

Dear (name of invitee),

As we have indicated in our communication over the past several months, (name of parish) is moving forward with a number of initiatives—most of which will focus on developing the many resources of our parish. As part of this initiative, we are pleased to announce that we are beginning a formal planning process in the area of Catholic Parish Development. We define Catholic development as "*the meaningful involvement of people in our mission and vision for the future.*" One of the major components of this process will be to form a development advisory council (DAC) that will meet three times and help create a strategic plan for our development, communication, total stewardship, and people engagement efforts. This is an exciting and challenging undertaking that will involve many people in an organized planning initiative.

We would like to personally invite you to participate in this challenging process as a member of the development advisory council. The (name of parish) core team specifically identified you to participate in this dynamic group because of the unique insights and perspective we feel you have to offer about our parish.

The date of our first meeting is on (date) at (time) in (place).

We have enclosed a copy of the agenda for our first meeting, along with the purpose and goals of the development advisory council and the challenges we will seek to solve. In addition, here are the dates, times, and places of all three meetings:

- Date of meeting #1
- Date of meeting #2
- Date of meeting #3

It would be very helpful if you could let us know if you will be able to participate so that we can adequately plan for our meetings. Please respond via phone call to the parish office (phone number) or by e-mail (e-mail address). In addition, someone from our core team will be personally reaching out to see if you have any questions. Hopefully, you will be able to work with us for these three meetings as we shape the future of the development, communication, total stewardship, and people engagement efforts here at (name of parish).

Thank you for your consideration, and we look forward to seeing you!

Sincerely,
(Pastor)

VI. FACILITATORS AND SCRIBES

In the beginning of the process, we talked about the core team members serving three roles: 1. Educating; 2. Facilitating; 3. Implementing. Now it is time for facilitation. After you agree upon the 6–8 challenges, core team members will need to divide up two by two—one or two can facilitate and one or two can scribe for each small group. It will be important to prepare for 5–6 small groups.

Please emphasize that core team members are being asked to facilitate and scribe and not to participate with their opinions. That is done in the core team meetings.

VII. THE CATHOLIC PARISH DEVELOPMENT STRATEGIC PLANNING PROCESS

Logistics In order to prepare for the development advisory council meetings, there are logistical items that need to be in place. Many of these are listed here.

- Handouts (agendas, individual information sheet for attendees to fill in key information about themselves—name, address, cell phone, e-mail, etc.)
- Nametags and pens
- One large meeting area
- 5–6 breakout rooms for each small group
- Audiovisual equipment for any PowerPoint presentations
- Refreshments
- Flip charts and markers

DAC Meeting #1 The core team should meet one hour before each DAC meeting. They should go over the agenda for the evening and discuss activities in each small group. Please keep in mind that each small group will seek to solve *all* of the challenges.

The first meeting is a bit different from all the other meetings. This meeting is built around five words:

- Introduction,
- Orientation,
- Education,
- Resources,
- Mission.

At this first meeting, all attendees will *introduce* themselves and let people know how long they have been in the parish and what activities/ministries they may be involved in.

At this first meeting, everyone should be *oriented* on what they will do and what has already been done. That way, everyone will get a good idea about the overall process.

It is always good to have a PowerPoint presentation that will *educate*—step by step—the parts of the planning process and show what happens meeting to meeting and what role everyone is invited to play.

There will be *resources* that should be provided and these are usually going to be the results of the parish-wide survey.

At this first meeting, you should hand out the present draft of the *Mission/Vision Statement(s)*.

Please make sure you know who will be the facilitators and scribes for the 5–6 small groups and which room each group will be in. Those breakout rooms should be set up with flip chart paper and markers available.

Because all teams will be solving all of the challenges, the best way to divide up the large group into teams is by a random count off. Whoever is facilitating the large group meeting (possibly a core team member) should simply count off, "Number 1, 2, 3, 4, 5; number 1, 2, 3, 4, 5." After everyone has been counted (not including the facilitators and scribes), you can indicate that the "ones" should go together, the "twos" go together, etc. The facilitator should then send them out to their breakout areas.

Agendas for the Three Development Advisory Council Meetings
Development Advisory Council Meeting #1
- Opening prayer
- Introductions
- Purpose and goals of the development advisory council
  - » To understand Catholic Parish Development
  - » To understand the parish's current communication,

development, total stewardship and people engagement efforts

» To help create strategies that will build a strategic plan for communications, development, total stewardship, and people engagement

» To prioritize the key action strategy solutions to the challenges

» To help implement the key strategies for those who wish to be further involved

» To accomplish the above by attending three meetings

- State of the parish message from the pastor
- Understanding Catholic Parish Development
- Overview of the planning process
- Work flow
- Challenges in the planning process
- Small-group work
    » Understanding of challenges
    » "First Sweep" of strategic solutions (brainstorming)
    » Should be written on the flip chart paper—challenge by challenge
- Future meeting dates
- Closing prayer

NOTE

In between the meetings, you should send a recap of the work of each of the small teams to the members of that team. Remember, during the first meeting, each team is brainstorming solutions for each of the challenges. At the first meeting, you should capture the names and contact information (by teams) from each person on the DAC and make that available to the facilitators and scribes.

Development Advisory Council Meeting #2

- Opening prayer
- Purposes and goals
- Recap of meeting #1
- Challenges in the planning process
- Small-group assignments for first-time participants
- Small-group work
  - » Review work from first meeting
  - » Complete "First Sweep" (brainstorming) of the strategic solutions for all challenges
- Next meeting date
- Closing prayer

NOTE

In between DAC meetings #2 and #3, each team should be sent the work they did in meeting #2. Please send each team only their work and not the work of the other teams.

Development Advisory Council Meeting #3 (final meeting)

- Opening prayer
- Recap of meeting #2
- Challenges in the planning process
- Small-group work
  - » Review your work from meeting #2
  - » Complete the brainstorming "sweep" of all challenges
  - » Convert the brainstorming "ideas" into strategic solutions
  - » 2–3 strategic solutions per challenge (quality not quantity)
  - » Use SMART formula
    S = Strategic
    M = Measurable
    A = Achievable
    R = Relevant
    T = Time-driven
  - » Begin each strategic solution with an action verb

- Large-group sharing (10 minutes)
- Each small group presents the number one challenge they believe should be implemented first.
- Discuss parish convocation
- The entire parish is invited to come for one evening and offer their solutions to the 6–8 challenges.
- DAC multi-vote (Please see "The Multi-Vote Process" explanation later in this lesson.)
- DAC evaluation/input sheet (Sample provided below).
- Closing prayer

VIII. THE CATHOLIC PARISH DEVELOPMENT CONVOCATION

After the third and final DAC meeting, it is time to invite the entire parish to the convocation (parish assembly) and ask them to solve the challenges. Promotion for the convocation can come from the pastor, the core team visits to the ministries, flyers, signs, bulletin inserts, website promotion, etc. The key here is to make sure everyone knows the challenges that you are asking people to solve in their parish.

One of the areas of confusion deals with the purpose of the convocation. The two questions (with answers) we hear all the time are:

1. If the development advisory council teams have solved the challenges already, why do you want more people to come in and offer their solutions?
   - Two reasons: Buy-in and ownership, and more creativity

2. Are you going to show the people who attend the convocation the solutions that the DAC came up with?
   - No. If we show the people coming to the convocation that we already have strategic solutions, they may ask themselves why they should get involved if this has already been done.

You then will end up with two sets of solutions—those from the DAC and those from the convocation. I suggest that you place more emphasis on the DAC strategic solutions because these teams spent more hours on this plan; however, we always see the "golden nuggets" that no one ever thought about that come out in the convocation, along with affirmation of the solutions already created. (Imitation is the greatest form of flattery).

The derivation of the word convocation:

- convocation (n.) Late fourteenth century. "assembly of persons," from Old French *convocation* and directly from Latin *convocationem*, noun of action from past participle stem of *convocare* "to call together," from *com-* "together" + *vocare* "to call," from *vox* "voice."
- We like the word and explanation: *When a community sends out invitations and rallies all of its people together to have a meeting to discuss pressing issues and challenges, this is a convocation.*

As stated earlier, the specific focus is to invite all parish families and ask them to *solve the challenges*. Generally speaking, this allows the people involved with the planning process to update people, seek buy-in through participation, gather the participants' best wisdom, and at the end of the convocation to let people know where this process is going.

In preparation for the convocation, a promotion committee should have used every communication angle as possible. In some parishes, we have seen a convocation phone committee of 20–30 people, who randomly select and call parish families for a week or two before the convocation. The two pieces we strongly suggest are: to make sure everyone in the parish is invited in some way, and to make sure that everyone in the parish sees the challenges that have been created in advance of the convocation.

The convocation is a two-hour event (except when parishes have an additional morning convocation, and then those are usually one hour because of lower attendance, and everyone can remain in the same gathering area).

The main question we receive is: If 5–6 small teams took three meetings to solve 6–8 challenges, how can a small group at the convocation solve all of these challenges in an hour? They cannot. What we find is that when broken into small groups, each group will be asked to look at all of the challenges and select those that resonate the most with them. Let's say we have 200 people at a convocation and we break into 15 small groups, and each group is asked to solve the challenges. We have found that most groups can offer viable and meaningful solutions to 4–5 challenges within an hour's time. And these 4–5 challenges are usually the most important to that small group and (interestingly) the most important to the parish. In addition, if we have 10–15 small groups and many of them "tackle" the same challenges (because of those challenges being important to that small group) then that is making a statement about those challenges that are addressed the most—they are important to solve.

In advance of the convocation, a number of logistical items need to be addressed:
- 15 facilitators and scribes
- Large gathering area
- 15 breakout rooms
- Nametags (numbered from 1–15 indicating which small group that person will serve in)
- Pens/pencils
- Signs directing where people should go when they break out into small groups
- Greeters
- One flip chart with markers
- 4 counters for the multi-vote process
- Handouts (agenda, individual input sheet/evaluation sheet)

Here is a sample agenda for a convocation.

THE STRATEGIC PLAN FOR PARISH DEVELOPMENT

XYZ Catholic Parish Convocation Agenda

LARGE-GROUP SETTING

1. Opening Prayer

2. Understanding the Planning Process
- Developing and advancing a Catholic parish
- Core team formation
- *Update* bulletin
- Parish planning team
- Mission
- Challenges–strategic solutions
- Convocation

3. Introduction of Parish Development Challenges

4. Instructions on Solving the Challenges

5. Introduction of Small-Group Facilitators/Scribe

6. Small-Group Work
- Introductions
- Clarification of challenges
- Assignment: Solve the challenges

LARGE-GROUP SETTING

7. Multi-Vote Process with All
(see The Multi-Vote Process below)

8. Where Do We Go from Here?

9. Closing Prayer

IX. EVALUATION/INPUT SHEETS

In this planning process, it will be important to hear from both the development advisory council (including the core team) and those who attend the convocation. Here is a sample evaluation sheet that should give you valuable information with regard to the effectiveness of the process, the prioritization of challenges, and a listing of who is interested in helping implement.

INDIVIDUAL INPUT SHEET

1. Please rate the overall planning process.

☐ Excellent   ☐ Very Good   ☐ Good   ☐ Fair   ☐ Not Valuable

2. Please rate the effectiveness of the following components of the planning process.

	HIGH					LOW
Agenda Items	5	4	3	2	1	0
Small-Group Effectiveness	5	4	3	2	1	0
Large-Group Presentations	5	4	3	2	1	0
Multi-Vote Process	5	4	3	2	1	0

3. Please name the top challenge you would recommend to be implemented over the next twelve months.

4. ☐ If you would like to work with the implementation of this strategic plan, please check here and write your name at the bottom.

5. Any overall comments?

Name _____

Address _____

City _____   Zip _____

Phone (H)_____   (C)_____

E-mail_____

Please use the back of this sheet to offer any further suggestions/comments.

X. THE MULTI-VOTE PROCESS

One of the best ways to prioritize challenges or any list of items for that matter is to use what is known as multi-voting. This is a Total Quality Management tool.

Purpose: To take a list and get a priority order

Reason: Quick and time-effective. It also allows everyone to get something.

Uses: Small- and large-group work that requires prioritization.

Process to Get Priority Order

1. Write all of the challenges on a separate flip chart. Please see below

   _____ Challenge #1
   _____ Challenge #2
   _____ Challenge #3
   _____ Challenge #4
   _____ Challenge #5
   _____ Challenge #6
   _____ Challenge #7
   _____ Challenge #8

2. Divide the number of items by 1/2. For example, with eight challenges, then it would be four. If you have an odd number like seven, divide in half and bump it up one. For example, it would be four.

3. Tell each member of your group that they are to select that number from the list. Say, "Out of these eight challenges, I want you to select the four that you would like to see implemented first."

4. After everyone has done this, then go down the list and ask, "How many voted for #1? How many voted for #2?"

5. Write the number of votes in the blank line in front of the challenge.

6. This will get all items in priority order.

XI. THE WRITTEN STRATEGIC PLAN
FOR PARISH DEVELOPMENT

After the convocation, the core team should work together to draft the strategic plan for development. The priority suggestions of which challenges to address first should come from five barometers:

- Discussion with core team members
- Evaluating/Input Sheets from the development advisory council
- Multi-Vote from the development advisory council
- Evaluation/Input sheets from the convocation
- Multi-Vote from the convocation

Usually, with the above barometers, it becomes evident what the top 2–3 challenges are.

The main focus is to fully understand the strategic solutions for each challenge that come from the development advisory council and from the convocation. The core team should discuss the challenges from the perspective of what is important in the short term (within one year) and what is important in the long term (within two to five years).

The components of the plan should cover the following:

- Parish mission and vision,
- Background on the planning process,
- Listing of core team members and development advisory council members,
- Steps in the process,
- Listing of challenges,
- Challenges and strategic solutions,
- Priorities.

The core team should present the final strategic plan for development to the pastor and parish council. None of this should be a surprise to anyone, because the pastor has served on the executive committee and the parish council has been represented on the core team from the very beginning.

XII. IMPLEMENTATION OF THE STRATEGIC PLAN FOR DEVELOPMENT

We find that the implementation of the priorities of the strategic plan can be handled in one of three ways:

1. There already is a staff person, ministry, council, etc., in place that can take this strategic action item over and implement it;
2. There is a staff person in place in this area; however, she/he needs help from an implementation team to make sure this priority is addressed;
3. There is nothing in place, and the implementation team takes on this priority.

Listed here are the steps and the forms for implementation.

IMPLEMENTATION PROCESS
Strategic Plan for Development and Stewardship
Steps for Success

Step 1: Accept the position of chair or implementation team member for one of the implementation teams. Note:

- The executive committee should establish implementation teams chairs;
- With the executive committee being the drivers of this strategic plan for development, they should also macro-manage the overall implementation process;
- A strategic plan coordinator should also be put in place that can manage the day-to-day flow of activities and the internal as well as external communication;
- The chairs for each of the implementation teams should primarily come from the core team, which is made up of parish leaders;

- The implementation team (not chairs) membership should come from the following:
  - » Core team members who are not chairs,
  - » Development advisory council (people who attended the workshops),
  - » Convocation attendees,
  - » Interested stakeholders (parishioners).

Step 2: Fully understand the roles and responsibilities of being a team member by doing the following:
- Attending key meetings,
- Reading the information provided,
- Asking any and all questions—at any time,
- Participating in the implementation of key challenges,
- Communicating progress/activities to team members.

Step 3: Understand the challenge(s) and strategic solution(s) you will begin to work with first.
- Executive committee input

Step 4: Understand how the challenge(s) with which you will be working interacts with the other challenges being implemented in other areas.

Step 5: Clearly understand the language and the roles (implementation logistics):
- Executive committee (with input from the chairs) decides on which challenge to address first for each implementation team;
- EC makes suggestions to chairs of implementation teams on possible solutions to consider in solving a challenge;
- Chairs of implementation teams decide on final solutions to use to solve challenges based on:
  - » EC suggestions,
  - » Strategic solutions from the strategic plan for development,

- Chairs meet with implementation teams and discuss implementation steps for the prioritized solutions;
- Forms are filled out, work begins, progress is tracked, and success is reported every six months.

Step 6: Invite others to join your team beyond whom you have already invited.

Step 7: Organize and orient your implementation team at the first official meeting.
- Training and education
- Focus of the implementation team
- Completion of forms
- Confirm meeting schedule

Step 8: Understand the communication information that needs to be recorded and reported.

Step 9: Understand the correct steps to take for addressing the challenge(s) with which you will be working:
- Executive committee recommends prioritized challenge and suggests strategic solutions to implementation team chairs;
- Chairs of implementation teams finalize the strategic solutions;
- Implementation teams decide on implementation steps;
- Implementation teams fill in implementation chart/form;
- Implementation chart/form reviewed by executive committee;
- Executive committee provides recommendations/input;
- Implementation chart/form goes back to implementation team with action recommended.

Step 10: Begin implementation—action items.

Step 11: Communicate team activities via forms.

Step 12: Pray for and celebrate success.

STRATEGIC PLAN FOR PARISH DEVELOPMENT
IMPLEMENTATION AREA REQUEST FORM

Implementation Team _____

Challenge/Goal _____

Chairs _____

Date _____

Statement of the Challenge/Goal:

☐ No Cost   ☐ Funding Required   _____ Approx. Cost

Estimated Dates:

Start _____   Complete _____

Person(s) Responsible _____

Specific solutions your team will use to solve this challenge:

☐ Project Approved   ☐ Project Rejected   ☐ Project Amended

Executive Committee Comments:

STRATEGIC PLAN FOR PARISH DEVELOPMENT
IMPLEMENTATION PROCESS

Meeting Summary Form

Date of Meeting _____

Implementation Team _____

Chairs _____

Members (present) _____

_____

_____

Members (absent) _____

_____

_____

- -

I. Agenda (attached)

II. Key discussion items

III. Key decisions made

IV. Action items for next meeting

V. Next meeting date

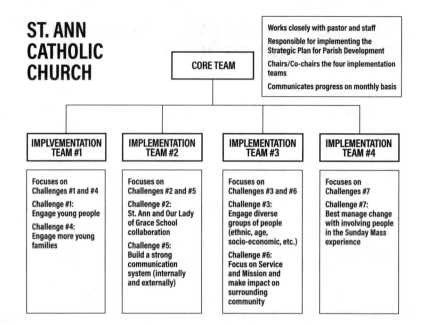

ST. ANN CATHOLIC CHURCH

CORE TEAM

Works closely with pastor and staff

Responsible for implementing the Strategic Plan for Parish Development

Chairs/Co-chairs the four implementation teams

Communicates progress on monthly basis

IMPLVEMENTATION TEAM #1

Focuses on Challenges #1 and #4

Challenge #1: Engage young people

Challenge #4: Engage more young families

IMPLEMENTATION TEAM #2

Focuses on Challenges #2 and #5

Challenge #2: St. Ann and Our Lady of Grace School collaboration

Challenge #5: Build a strong communication system (internally and externally)

IMPLEMENTATION TEAM #3

Focuses on Challenges #3 and #6

Challenge #3: Engage diverse groups of people (ethnic, age, socio-economic, etc.)

Challenge #6: Focus on Service and Mission and make impact on surrounding community

IMPLEMENTATION TEAM #4

Focuses on Challenges #7

Challenge #7: Best manage change with involving people in the Sunday Mass experience

NOTE

The above chart is from St. Ann Catholic Church in the Archdiocese of Cincinnati. This is the organizational structure that is being used to implement their strategic plan for parish development.

XIII. THE RELATIONSHIP OF THE IMPLEMENTATION TEAMS AND THE ALREADY EXISTING PARISH COUNCIL AND ITS COMMISSIONS AND COMMITTEES.

In 2018, ISPD worked with Father Jim Manning (see Lesson Two) at St. Mary of the Assumption Parish in Springboro, Ohio. The process we followed is the exact same process that is outlined in this lesson. There was an excellent core team in place; we had over 150 people involved in the planning process; and when it came time for implementation, four teams were formed. They have made huge strides and accomplished so much in the area of parish development. One of the questions that came up early in the implementation stage was this: How do the implementation teams differ from the parish council and the commissions? Isn't this going to be a duplication of efforts? Father Jim provided a wonderful explanation that I would like to share. This, as we say, comes from a pastor and a parish that "get it."

> The parish council represents the "voice of the people" all of the time. The implementation teams represent the "voice of the people" that emerged from the Catholic Parish Development (CPD) strategic planning process in the short term. The CPD planning process conducted by ISPD normally has three phases: 1) a pipelining stage where the input of parishioners is invited; 2) a planning stage that results from the input of parishioners; and 3) an implementation stage. Implementation teams are formed to implement the outcomes of the planning process. It is important to understand how this CPD strategic planning process interfaces with the work of the parish council.
>
> One, when an implementation team, in discussion with the pastor, believes that parish council and its commissions/committees are doing a good job in representing the voice of the people and are already implementing similar initiatives, the implementation team simply affirms the work of the council and stays out of their way. Two, when the implementation team believes, in discussion with the pastor, that the parish council and its commissions/committees need help, they offer the needed assistance and work with the parish council. Three, when the parish council and its commissions/committees do not have the time, talent, or energy to implement a strategic initiative, the implementation team takes over the project. A good example is a capital campaign. Parish council and its commissions/committees would not have the time, energy, or talent to conduct such a process. The implementation team takes this over for the good of the parish. Another example would be the phone outreach ministry. The parish council and its commissions/committees would not have the time to personally call every family in the parish three times per year and invite them to something and also check to see how they are doing. The implementation team launches this effort.

Another example would be working with Habitat for Humanity. The parish council would not have the time or the resources to spend a number of weekends building a home in coordination with Habitat for Humanity. The implementation team can make this a parish project and rally parish families to help.

The implementation teams thus enable the parish council and its commissions/committees to help the pastor manage the ordinary details of the parish by taking on short-term initiatives that the parish council is not equipped to do. The two can and should work together for the good of the parish and not hinder each other in the work that they both do.

XIV. VALUE OF THE ISPD STRATEGIC PLAN PROCESS FOR CATHOLIC PARISHES

Throughout the book, we talk about developing a Catholic parish through the meaningful involvement of people. *Belonging leads to believing.* So many of the measurements that we use in terms of success deal with people engagement:

- How many people accepted the invitation to serve on the core team as a team player and become involved in the process?
- How many people took the parish survey?
- How many ministries were able to be visited by core team members?
- How many people accepted the invitation to serve on the development advisory council and did so with consistency and quality?
- How many people attended the convocation and participated in a meaningful manner?
- How many people raised their hand and offered to serve on one of the implementation teams?
- How many people are serving on an implementation team?

To develop and advance a Catholic parish is a major challenge. We have always believed that it is all about people and how well we are able to engage them, whether through the planning process or through the implementation of key strategic initiatives.

To review, the 7 "I"s will come alive if we follow the process and believe in it.

If this planning and implementation process for Catholic Parish Development can serve as a catalyst to improve the parish and its culture of engagement and also bring people closer to Christ, and Christ closer to people, then we believe it will be successful.

Questions, Exercises, and Next Best Steps for Lesson Eleven

1. Please list the people in your parish who would serve on the executive committee for this strategic plan for development process.

2. Please list the ministries or groups in your parish who meet on a regular and consistent basis. These would be the ministries/groups that core team members would visit to introduce and then update on the progress of the strategic plan for development process.

3. In terms of introducing this strategic plan for parish development process to the parish, please outline what you (pastor, core team member, other parish leader) would say from the pulpit at all Masses. You can use the words, phrases, and suggestions from this lesson in order to create your outline.

4. Please create the 6–8 DRAFT challenges that you would want to bring to the development advisory council to solve. Please remember the focus of this process is on parish development.

- Challenge 1
- Challenge 2
- Challenge 3
- Challenge 4
- Challenge 5
- Challenge 6
- Challenge 7
- Challenge 8

5. In moving forward with your strategic plan for parish development, please outline an approximate timeline of when you will have the following components in place.

- Establishment of the executive committee
  By (date) _____

- Establishment of the core team
  By (date) _____

- Parish-wide survey
  By (date) _____

- Introduction of parish development and the planning process to the parish
  By (date) _____

- Creation of the 6–8 challenges
  By (date) _____

- Visits to key ministries begin
  By (date) _____

- Establishment of the development advisory council
  By (date) _____

- DAC Meeting 1
  By (date) _____

- DAC Meeting 2
  By (date) _____

- DAC Meeting 3
  By (date) _____

- Parish Convocation
  By (date) _____

- Final Strategic Plan for Parish Development
  By (date) _____

- Implementation Begins
  By (date) _____

Lesson Twelve: "Hire" the Parish Development Director

In the same way, let your light shine before others, so that they may see your good works and give glory to your Father who is in heaven. MATTHEW 5:16

For many parishes, "hiring" a development director has never crossed their mind. There are many reasons for that, with the two top ones being finances and lack of understanding of what a parish development director would do. We have never recommended putting this person in place on the front end of the development efforts; however, it is important when a parish does decide to move forward with development that there is a person who raises his/her hand and says, "I am responsible for parish development!" In the beginning, this may be the pastor, a staff member, a core team member, or a capable volunteer. Whether or not the parish moves into hiring someone part-time or full-time greatly depends on the importance parish leaders place on this ministry. Please remember: someone must shine the light for this ministry of parish development.

Throughout the book, there are many processes that do point to the need for a development director, and as we said, this could be part-time, full-time, or a volunteer effort. One of the best parish development directors I have ever worked with was a retired business owner who brought a great deal of experience in "customer service" and communications.

As you ponder what to do to fill this position, there are a number of questions to consider:

- When is the right time to bring this person on board?
- What should the job description look like?
- Do we hire from within or go outside of our parish?
- What should be the focus areas for this person?
- How do we get the word out that we are looking for a director?
- How much do we pay?
- Where will we put this person?
- What kind of equipment, supplies, and materials will this person need?
- How will the parish development director interact with other leadership groups?
- What kind of person are we looking for?

Regardless of who or when, let's examine more closely the role of the parish development director. In a "perfect world," what would we want this person responsible for? We do know that one of the main traps is that, over a period of time, the development office can become a "dumping ground" for everything that no one else wants to do. If development is going to thrive, then we recommend that this person stick to the job description.

Below is a sample job description. Please feel free to amend, edit, and change. It does cover the main areas of a comprehensive effort.

DIRECTOR OF PARISH DEVELOPMENT JOB DESCRIPTION

Purpose of Position: To take a leadership role in the parish by implementing the development activities and processes, including development office management, strategic planning, total stewardship process, financial resource development, people engagement, and public relations/communications

Reports to: Pastor

Major Responsibilities:

A. In the area of development day-to-day management
   1. To maintain a development office and organize all development activities.
   2. To update and maintain donor/database records of all publics.
   3. To put together the development core team to work alongside the parish development efforts.
   4. To actively work with
      » Clergy,
      » Parish staff,
      » Core team,
      » Parish council,
      » Ministry leaders,
      » Parishioners.

B. In the area of parish revenue
   1. To set up and implement a financial leadership process
   2. To set up and implement a planned giving process

C. In the area of public relations and communication
   1. To serve as one of the public relations agent for the parish.
   2. To promote major parish events.
   3. To oversee a quarterly newsletter that will go out to all publics.

4. To oversee an annual report.
5. To design and implement a communications plan that will include
   » Bulletin communication about parish development,
   » Parish website,
   » Social media outlets for the parish,
   » Parish app,
   » E-mail communication.
6. To organize the new parishioner welcome process.

D. In the area of special event fund/friend-raising:
   1. To coordinate all special events.
   2. To empower volunteers to participate fully in special events.
   3. To prepare a master plan for all development $$$ and fund-raising $$$.

E. In the area of people engagement
   1. To follow the 7-"I" process of inviting and involving people in the mission and vision of the parish.
   2. To organize a vibrant volunteer program for the ministries of the parish.
   3. To set up an appreciation and affirmation plan for the parish.

F. In the area of total stewardship process: prayer, ministry and finance
   1. To plan, manage, and implement the total stewardship process of prayer, service, and finance
      » Timeline,
      » Publications,
      » Education and in-service,
      » Special events (ministry fair, ministry appreciation dinner),
      » Ministry volunteer organization,
      » Annual evaluation.

2. To identify, invite, and involve the total stewardship committee in the process

G. In the area of the written strategic plan for development
   1. To oversee the creation of the strategic plan for development.
   2. To ensure that hundreds of parishioners are invited to give input into the strategic plan for parish development
   3. To oversee the implementation of the strategic plan for development
   4. To communicate the progress of the strategic plan for development

Questions, Exercises, and Next Best Steps for Lesson Twelve

1. Please describe the traits you would look for in hiring a development director for your parish.

2. What would be the main areas you would want this person to work with in your parish? Please describe.

3. If your parish is not ready to hire a development director (part-time or full-time), please list 3–5 people in your parish you would consider inviting to coordinate the parish development efforts.

4. Why do you believe it is important to have a person who is "in charge" of parish development? Please explain.

5. What measurements would you use in your parish to determine if this person (paid or volunteer) is successful in his/her role as parish development director?

Lesson Thirteen: Research Best Practices in Catholic Parish Development

|| "Where there is no guidance, a people falls, but in an abundance of counselors there is safety." PROVERBS 11:14

Through the years, we have had the wonderful opportunity to work with hundreds of parishes throughout the country. These parishes saw, and still see, the value of having an active and formal parish development effort in place. They all went through the steps we have thus far described in the book, and mainly, they created their own strategic plan for parish development. In this lesson, I would like to offer some best practices. St. Lads in the Diocese of Cleveland shared many of their people engagement processes. Listed here are also some best practices from other parishes addressing the challenges of parishioner welcome, reaching those not involved but registered, involving young people, implementing total stewardship, partnering the parish and the school, communicating with all parishioners, keeping track of all parish families, launching a capital campaign, running special events, setting up a planned giving process, and more.

Many of these strategic initiatives come from St. Mary of the Assumption Parish in Springboro, Ohio; St. Anthony of Padua in The Woodlands, Texas; Our Lady of Perpetual Help Parish in Belle Chasse, Louisiana; and St. Ann Parish in Cincinnati, Ohio.

As we always say, it is important to realize that what works in one parish may not work in another; however, it does not hurt to recognize and acknowledge best practices. At the root of all of these action strategies is the belief that this is all about the *meaningful involvement of people in your mission and vision for the future.*

CATHOLIC PARISH DEVELOPMENT BEST PRACTICES

- Establish a communications committee to evaluate current communications and information gathering of parishioners. Develop a plan using IT and social media to improve communication with all members and all age groups of the parish. Committee could be 6–10 people.
- Survey all parishioners to determine their preferred method(s) of communication.
- Explore further ways of improvement through a self-evaluation of the website. In his book *Transforming Parish Communications*, Scot Landry offers an evaluation tool: Rate Your Parish Website.
- Create a new parishioner welcoming committee of 15–20 parishioners who will personally connect with each new family, beginning with a welcoming phone call, personal home visit, and an invitation to be part of a parish "connect group."
- Implement a Mass welcoming subcommittee for each Mass to volunteer to welcome parishioners as they enter church. Key strategies at Mass could be:
  » Subcommittee members directing people to a welcome/registration desk;
  » Having guest books available to capture information;
  » Have "connect cards" to hand out to those seeking information or needing help of any kind. (Please refer to the lesson on "The Warm Church.")
- Create a survey to be given to new parishioners within the first year, asking about their orientation into the parish. This could provide some valuable information as to the needs and wants of newcomers.
- Conduct a parishioner survey of daily and weekend Masses in order to test parishioner attitudes on the sound system, music, welcoming, participation, and reverence in order to provide feedback on the overall Sunday Mass experience.

- Establish a committee to explore best practices of other Catholic and non-Catholic churches and what they do to invite and also retain parishioners of all ages.
- Establish a parish library in order to make publications available to parishioners from leading Catholic authors and speakers, such as Father James Mallon (*Divine Renovation*), Father Michael White and Tom Corcoran (*Rebuilt, Tools for Rebuilding*, and *Rebuilding Your Message*), Matthew Kelly (*The Four Signs of a Dynamic Catholic*), and Scot Landry (*Transforming Parish Communications*).
- Parish council, parish staff, and ministry leaders should be encouraged to view *The Amazing Parish* website. Taught through their conferences and resources, plus referred to by several key Catholic leaders seeking to help transform parishes, the seven traits of an amazing parish are worth noting as the parish moves forward:
  » A real leadership team,
  » Clear vision,
  » Reliance on prayer,
  » An awesome Sunday experience,
  » Compelling formation,
  » Small-group discipleship,
  » Missionary zeal.
- Establish social media accounts (Twitter, Facebook, Snapchat, etc.) with information on parish activities provided by the youth group, parish organizations, and the pastor.
- With the parish growing each year, conduct a demographic survey/census to anticipate growth over the next several years.
- Create a social/activities committee composed of people in this target age group (18–35) in order to offer, implement, and promote social and athletic events. Consider two groupings: college age and young families.
- Offer a Mass once per month geared to the age group (18–35) that would involve many of these individuals and their

families in the liturgy (ushers, presentation of the gifts, choir, readers, presentations, etc.).

- Organize a plan for current parishioners to host gatherings in their homes, inviting the neighbors and friends. Have pastor meet and greet.
- Create an outreach ministry team who will personally contact and invite all parish families—via telephone—quarterly, to include Christmas, Easter, fair, and spring picnic.
- Weekly, or biweekly, video (on a smart phone) the pastor or a parish leader talking about something exciting that is going on in the parish. Make the video no more than two minutes and e-mail it to all parish families.
- Create a survey directed toward PSR families that will help determine how they could be more involved in the parish and what could be done to encourage regular attendance and involvement.
- Encourage one person within each ministry, including the church and the school, to be responsible for providing information monthly to the church website. Establish within the website and bulletin the "Latest News" or "Needs" corner for ministries.
- Consider mailing the parish bulletin to those who do not attend Mass on a regular basis. Include other special handouts that promote the parish and the school and the parish app.
- Create a committee to organize an annual young adult conference at the parish with exciting speakers/musicians who will engage them with our faith.
- Continue and better integrate Flock Notes (communication software) with all parish families.
- Create a parish "Make a Difference Day" to assist needy parishioners and community members who need help with home repairs, yard work, and home modifications.
- Develop a parish-sponsored list of babysitters who have been trained, certified, and have parish character references. Make

the list available for in-home and on-site babysitting. Dedicate area for babysitting during Mass and parish events.

- Create a mothers of young children club to provide social activities, speakers, education, and support.
- Host a "Day of Culture" that reflects the various ethnic groups of the parish.
- Establish a parish service coordinator to organize service events (i.e., mission trips, helping St. Vincent de Paul, etc.) as a way to engage parishioners in helping others locally, nationally, and internationally.
- Organize a neighborhood outreach ministry, where geographic areas are divided into groups of approximately 50–100 families. Two or three neighborhood captains could coordinate and gather pertinent information on all of the Catholic families in that area. Social activities, home meetings, prayer groups, and parish communication are all part of this "divide and conquer" process. In addition to the above, the neighborhood outreach ministry is great for knowing who moves in and moves out (Catholic or not) so people can be welcomed by the parish. This ministry is also helpful in knowing when families need outreach, and for overall community building. This can begin small with several areas and then grow over a number of years.
- Offer "Educational Masses" where people are taught the meaning of the parts of the Mass.
- Provide materials, signs, logos, t-shirts, etc., so parishioners can identify their affiliation with the parish outside of the parish at community and neighborhood events.
- Create a parish brochure that is targeted to new families moving into the area; this would provide parish services, Mass times, and unique offerings. Distribute to welcome/visitor centers, real estate agencies, and human resource departments of corporations.
- At the end of Mass, have a ministry leader present a very short talk on a specific ministry—"A Minute for a Ministry."

- Highlight a different ministry every week in the newsletter, the bulletin, and on the website.
- Establish a leadership institute for growth opportunities for all Catholic leaders in the parish (and possibly beyond). The institute could be set up with online presentations through software programs like Go To Webinar, which can be attended live or taken through recordings. Some type of leadership certification could be established and mandated, so that so many hours could be earned by parish leaders. Some suggested topics are:
  » Traits of Successful Catholic Leadership,
  » Managing Change in a Catholic Parish,
  » Communication Vehicles and Skills,
  » Maximizing the Inclusion of Varying Ethnic Groups of the Parish,
  » How to Run a Meeting,
  » Assessing the Work of Catholic Ministries.

Questions, Exercises, and Next Best Steps for Lesson Thirteen

1. Name the parishes in your diocese and/or area where you could reach out and seek their best practices in people engagement.

2. From the many strategic initiatives listed above, name five that interest you the most.

3. Have the parish council and/or the core team research "The Amazing Parish" website over a month-long period of time. Dedicate two to three meetings where these parish leaders would discuss those areas that resonated the most. After these discussions, write down the ten most pertinent suggestions that could be applied to your parish.

4. Have the parish council and/or the core team read Father James Mallon's book *Divine Renovation* over a month-long period of time. Dedicate two to three meetings where these parish leaders would discuss those areas that resonated the most. After these discussions, write down the ten most pertinent suggestions that could be applied to your parish.

5. In terms of parish development, and as you view these best practices from other parishes, what is the one area that you believe should be addressed and improved in your parish? Please explain.

Lesson Fourteen: Remember That "People Fuel" Is the Overall Key to Success

|| "Make sure that every person, of whatever background, can find in you a welcoming heart." POPE BENEDICT XVI

If we believe that parish development is all about people, then it becomes extremely important that we set up our efforts using the 7 "I"s. Through this engagement, we can then position, educate, and invite people to live as stewards for life.

Look at the parish organizational structure diagram in Lesson Six, and note the box labeled "People Fuel." This is essential to success. Through the years we have developed a number of ways to fuel the parish with people. Some of these ways are one-time efforts, and other ways are meant to have people serve for an extended period of time. Regardless, the outcome should always be the same: building a strong sense of ownership by developing meaningful relationships with as many people as possible. As we have said over and over: *belonging leads to believing*, and successful parish development brings people to Christ and Christ to people.

Listed here—with a brief description—are some ways that parishes can invite and involve their various constituencies. The key to inviting and involving is that you do it all the time. You must always invite people—especially new people who are not presently involved with you—to participate in something, however big or small.

We encourage pastors, development directors, and all parish leaders to set a goal each year to invite and involve 100 new people. Whom to invite? Let's take a look at some of the people you need to have on your database:

- Parishioners,
- Parish leadership groups,
- Parish staff,
- Parents (if applicable),
- Former parishioners,
- Business community,
- Neighbors,
- Feeder sources,
- Financial leaders to your parish,
- Corporations and foundations,
- Civic, political, and cultural leaders in your community.

Can you imagine the value of having this list of people—along with notes and annotated information about many of them?

PROCESSES TO ENGAGE PEOPLE (SOME REFERRED TO IN OTHER LESSONS IN THE BOOK)

Parish Development Core Team This is our term, and we refer to the core team as a group of 15–18 people who work hand in hand with the parish development efforts in implementing the day-to-day activities.

Positive, committed, and mission/vision-driven, they usually serve for 6–12 months, meeting on a weekly or biweekly basis.

Personal Interviews This is an excellent way for a pastor or parish leader to invite people for a short 20–30-minute interview and let them get involved with giving their opinions and thoughts.

Development Advisory Committee (DAC) In helping a parish set up their development efforts, one of the main processes is to create a written strategic plan for development. This requires three meetings of some 60–80 people.

We recommend using the 60%–40% rule here. The core team should invite 60% "new" people (those not involved) and 40% "old" people (those already involved).

Surveys and Questionnaires This is a highly effective method of getting people involved. Surveys and questionnaires allow a person to write opinions and make suggestions.

This heightens interest, and the people who are asked to fill these out take a greater interest in what the results are and what is happening in the parish.

Input Sessions This is a process where people are invited to a 50–55-minute input session. This usually involves a random selection of parishioners, and three questions are asked:

- What impresses you about the parish?
- What are those areas where we need the most improvement?
- As you look to the future, what would you like to see in the next 1–3–5 years and beyond?

Convocation At the end of a planning process, we encourage parishes to invite all parish families to a convocation (assembly) where people can provide solutions to parish challenges.

Committee/Commission/Ministry Already in Place One of the key focus areas of any development effort is to make sure you invite participation from those groups, committees, ministries, and commissions that are already in place. Visits and updates provided to the parish council, the education commission, the finance committee, etc., are very important. While there, the development "point person" can invite these people to be part of a convocation, come to an input session, serve on a planning committee, etc.

Publication Evaluation Committee In every parish there are always 5–10 people who have expertise in graphic design, journalism, or communications and public relations. One method of involving these folks is to invite them to serve on an *ad hoc* committee that would meet once or twice. Their goal would be to evaluate and offer a fresh, new perspective on the parish publication materials—newsletters, bulletins, brochures, stationery, etc.

Pastor Cabinet One method of inviting key leaders, who do not have the time to serve on standing boards and committees, is to have the pastor begin a cabinet of people. This cabinet would meet twice per year for lunch or breakfast and offer advice on future direction of the parish. This cabinet—usually 10–20 in number—would be made up of key influential leaders who do not have a lot of time but do want to get involved.

Informational Sessions When something exciting is going on in the parish, it is a great idea to invite parishioners to informational sessions where these new exciting things can be explained (new site master plan for buildings, new communication plan for the parish, new small faith communities program for the parish, etc.).

New Parishioner Welcome Committee Key group for parish development—this committee should be made up of parishioners who have been in the parish for less than a year as well as those who have been there for a while.

The task here is to create successful ways to invite and involve new parishioners in the parish.

Total Stewardship Committee Obviously, this group concentrates on the total stewardship efforts of the parish.
- Stewardship of prayer
- Stewardship of ministry
- Stewardship of offering

Implementation Teams for the Strategic Plan When the strategic plan for parish development is ready for implementation, there need to be implementation teams who can take this over and begin the work.

Mission/Vision Statement Committee This group is 5–8 people who put together the drafts of a mission statement and vision statement.

One-on-One "Cup of Coffee" Don't forget: one of the most effective ways to involve people is to sit across a table from them, have a cup of coffee, and invite them to be a part of this new vision for the future of your parish.

Neighborhood Networks There are some parishes throughout the country who have gotten very serious about communications, people involvement, and making sure they know who moves into their area. They have set up neighborhood networks, where every family in the parish is placed in a geographic area, and every geographic area has a captain or two.

Steering Committee for a Capital Campaign This is the group of 15–18 people who explore the viability and feasibility of conducting a capital campaign to build buildings or renovate or add on.

Capital Campaign Cabinet These are the chairs of the divisions of the capital campaign + the operational chairs of the campaign.

Planned Giving Committee This group of 10–15 people help establish a process for a parish to move forward with an organized planned giving effort.

Fund-Raising Event Committee This group of 6–8 people, representing all key areas of the parish, would be responsible for creating a master plan for fund-raising. No fund-raiser by any group could be held unless it met this group's approval and was put on a master calendar.

Home Receptions As part of the capital campaign strategies, campaign leaders are invited to host receptions in their home in order to gather a small group of people to invite their financial participation.

Saving the Best for Last: One-on-One Relationship Building Today Catholic parishes are faced with challenges that are quite daunting. Every week, as we consult and teach throughout the country, we see these challenges knocking many Catholic institutions back on their heels, and even some of them out of the total picture. We all know what they are:

- Lack of parishioner involvement;
- Parishioners leaving the parish;
- Costs of running the parish;
- Consistency of leadership in our parishes;
- Changing demographics;
- Facility needs;
- Lack of a "people engagement" culture;
- Boss management vs. team management;
- Wanting dynamic change but doing the same things over and over again.

This is not to say that there are not Catholic parishes who are moving forward in a visionary and dynamic manner. Many solutions are being tried. Some of them work, and some of them do not.

Direct-mail campaigns, strategic planning efforts, better steward-ship processes, more fund-raising events, mergers, capital cam-paigns, new governance and operational models, business com-munity relationships/partnerships—the list goes on and on. And, interestingly, with the right leadership and direction, many of them work.

We would like to take this a step further and address a topic that we have talked about for more than 10 years. It is a topic that usually meets with two responses and then is quickly dismissed. Those two responses are:

- "Interesting."
- "Yeah, right. You must be out of your mind!"

Here is our belief: *In order for Catholic parishes to prevail and meet the daunting challenges we are facing in this new millennium, we must figure out the ways, means, and processes for parish leaders to meet with every parish family (one-on-one) at least once per year for a lengthy conversation, in their home or at the parish, "eyeball to eyeball."* Interesting! Yeah, right!

We understand the cost. We understand the logistics. We un-derstand the time commitment, and we understand the person-nel factor. However, if we really believe that *people engagement* and *meaningful involvement* are the most important beliefs in Catholic Parish Development, then we need to make this happen.

Let us say that your parish—over the next year—was able to recruit and train 8–10 teams, with 2 persons on each team. Sample combinations:

- Pastor and parish staff member
- Two parish staff members
- Pastor and parish council member
- Two parish council members
- Two finance council members
- Two ministry leaders
- Two parish leaders

Let us look at the conversation topics and the advantages of building the relationships with each and every parish family.

What the parish teams can discuss and share with parish family:

- Vision and plans for the future of the parish;
- Spiritual growth opportunities for all members of the family;
- Educational opportunities for all members of the family;
- Changes in the parish and how they will impact that family;
- How the parish operates;
- Ways of engagement and involvement that family members would enjoy;
- Discussion of the three gifts of prayer, involvement, and financial participation.

After bringing out the above, the parish team (of two) need to sit back and ask this question: *Mr. and Mrs. Johnson (or Ms. Johnson or Mr. Wilson or whatever), what we would like for you to do is share with us how (name of parish) can better serve you as your home parish and what we can do in order to continue to build a strong relationship in the future. What are your needs? How can we help you meet those needs? What gifts would you enjoy sharing with the parish? How can we help each of you in your spiritual journey?*

Now before we hit the panic button on this one, let's set some guidelines and state some basic tenets. We are not saying that this needs to be put in place next month. We are inviting you to begin serious discussions with your parish leaders about how this would be possible and why this would be so valuable.

As parish leaders, you may want to begin visiting with new families that move into your parish at the beginning of a calendar year. That would be almost unheard of in many Catholic parishes. Most of the time, we *react*. New families registering are asked to come to a coffee and donut gathering or some monthly new parish family function. We are saying that the first visit with the new family is the first step of many visits in the future as you chart the course for this family and their journey with you for many years to come.

In order to be perfectly clear: the goal here is to visit with *every* family in your parish once a year to engage in a meaningful conversation.

The advantages are overwhelming. Every new family in your parish would know from the get-go that this is the way you build your faith community—one by one. This would become the new norm. This would be the way that parish leaders could track progress from year to year. Naturally, forms will have to be created, files will have to be kept, and the most important component of all of this is *response*. The ability to respond to the needs of each family will mean the difference in success or failure.

This is setting up the parish operation with a *totally new modus operandi*. It is exciting, and the contacts, the resources, the relationships, and the connections have the potential to be unbelievable.

Before you begin to quickly dismiss, let's go back to the challenges and look at how this personal relationship building campaign can address the very concerns that keep Catholic leaders awake at night.

- Lack of parishioner involvement: This would be directly addressed in every conversation with the emphasis being on: *What would you enjoy sharing here at your parish?*
- Parishioners leaving the parish: This could be discussed with invitations for families to make referrals, and the personal visit certainly would be building a very strong retention action.
- Costs of running the parish: This could finally be explained in full—what the parish budget is, how it is managed, what is done with the money, why the offertory is important, why the parish annual fund is important, why gifts in kind are important, etc.
- Leadership in our parishes: this could surface many potential volunteer leaders for the parish.
- Changing demographics: The visiting team could learn many things about the area, the neighborhood, and the families living in that area.

- Facility needs of our parishes and schools: the case for support plus the identification of facilities needs could all be part of this conversation.
- Lack of a "people engagement" culture: with the family visits, this is exactly what you would be doing—engaging the family.
- Boss management vs. team management: it would be easily seen that the Catholic parish's management style is collaborative and inviting.
- Wanting dynamic change but doing the same things over and over again: this is major change.

So, what do we have to do to convince Catholic leaders to open up the discussions on this topic? This will vastly change the way we operate as Catholic parishes. This outreach can be integrated into our culture, and ten years from now we will not be saying, "How do we keep the doors open?" but, "Can you believe how strong of a faith community we have now that we have 'Opened Wide the Doors to Christ'?"

Obviously, there are other ways to invite and engage people in the life of your parish. As we have said before, please make sure you gather three key pieces of information:

1. The list of their gifts:
   - Areas of interest,
   - Areas of expertise,
   - Resource areas,
   - Hobbies,
   - What they would most like to do in given the opportunity.
2. Their e-mail address(es)
3. Their cell phone number(s)

In addition, here is a sample list of gifts that you may want to include in the packet of information when you seek people involvement.

Gifts of Wisdom, Expertise, Skill, and Talent That You Would Be Willing to Share Here at the Parish

AC/Heating expertise

Artist

Attorney

Auto mechanic

Background in public relations, marketing, and/or advertising

Bereavement counselor

Carpenter

Chef

Childcare

Circus Clown

Coach: Sport(s) _____

_____

Communications expertise

Cooking

Database management

Drama/Performing Arts

Driver

Electrician

Event planner

Financial advisor

Fitness instructor

Grant writer

Graphic design

Healthcare worker

Historian

Home visitor

Inventor

Landscaper

Law enforcement officer

Legal advisor

Musician

Organizer and cleaner

Painter

Performer

Photographer

Planning

Plumber

Public speaker

Real estate agent

Research analyst

Scientist

Secretarial skills

Self-protection expert

Small-group facilitator

Tax preparer

Teacher

Technology expert

Theater director

Videographer

Website designer

Woodworker

Word processor

Working with seniors

Writer

Other: _____

_____

Questions, Exercises, and Next Best Steps for Lesson Fourteen

For Lesson Fourteen, there is only one exercise: Over the next ninety days, have the pastor, the parish council, and the core team discuss the feasibility of implementing the **One-on-One Relationship Building** process.

Lesson Fifteen: Avoid and Correct the Fifteen Most Common Parish Development Mistakes

‖ "Yesterday is gone. Tomorrow has not yet come. We have only today. Let us begin." MOTHER TERESA

Before we go any further, we need to clarify what we mean by "mistakes." We are referring to those areas of Catholic Parish Development that we see as taking a wrong turn or making an incorrect approach. We feel sure there could be argument on both sides with some of these "mistakes"; however, we are electing to zero in on those areas we deem incorrect in both philosophy and action.

For example, over a year ago I was invited to make a presentation—along with three other consulting companies—to a Catholic parish who wanted to embark upon a capital campaign to raise $3,000,000 to build a new multipurpose building. We presented our "Traffic Light Process"—a proven method of approaching a capital campaign from a development stance rather than just a fund-raising stance. We stressed building support through input sessions, having a long-range pastoral plan in place (not just for the facilities but in all areas), having a core team trained and ready, publishing a Q & A booklet to explain what is going on, conducting a parish-wide survey at every Mass to determine attitudes, integrating a strong prayer component into the process, hosting a parish convocation to talk about vision and not just facilities, inviting 100 new people to the development effort each year, and so on. This parish had done some "pipe-lining" to their parish families, but only in the area of facilities—not vision, mission, ministry planning, or prayer.

They elected to go with another company who would conduct the feasibility study within 30–45 days and begin the fund-raising within 60–90 days. Unfortunately, they did not see the wisdom of taking a "development" approach to building their parish for the future. They simply wanted the money for the multipurpose building. The end.

To me, that approach was (and is) a mistake. We feel that there are certain steps you need to take in getting a parish ready for a capital campaign. Some of those steps were missed. Also, and probably the most important of all, there is a fantastic opportunity available in using a parish capital campaign as the springboard into future development of the parish—in all areas. Plus, a capital campaign is a wonderful time to evangelize and get to know so many new people. Many parishes miss out in not taking a development approach; they simply want to "get the money." We call that approach a mistake. Are there arguments on both sides? Sure. We have our belief set, and there are others who have their own.

Interestingly, that same parish that sought to raise $3.0 million did raise around $2.1 million, and when the campaign was over, they did not have any of the following in place:
- New parish leaders,
- New parish development office and officer,
- New parish families who felt part of the faith community,
- Renewed energy for parish ministries,
- Identifiable planned giving prospects,
- Written strategic plan for parish development for the next 3–5 years,
- Major donor process,
- Increased total stewardship process,
- New vision for the future.

Therefore, this final lesson in this section of the book is created to expose the most common mistakes *that we see as being incorrect—in philosophy and approach*.

MISTAKE #1: *Development efforts are launched, and the leadership of the parish does not understand the difference between development and fund-raising.*

Questions to ask to overcome the mistake:

- What education and training are available for the pastor and parish leaders to understand and learn what Catholic Parish Development is about?
- What in-service has been provided to parish leaders on the true meaning of Catholic Parish Development?
- Why did parish leaders want to first establish a Catholic Parish Development effort?
- Are there pastors in the diocese who do understand development? If so, would they be willing to come and speak with your pastor and other parish leaders?
- Do parish leaders understand the 7-"I" philosophy?
  » Identify-inform-invite-involve-implement-invest-improve
- How *Catholic* are your development efforts?

MISTAKE #2: *The development director's compensation and/or the success of the development effort is determined solely by the amount of money raised.*

Questions to ask to overcome the mistake:

- How much education have parish leaders had on what to expect from a development effort?
- How clear is the job description for the development director?
- What outcomes have been determined for the first year? The second year? The third year? The fourth year? The fifth year?
- Do most parish leaders understand that a true development effort takes 2–3 years to grow and mature?

MISTAKE #3: *There is no written strategic plan for parish development in place.*

Questions to ask to overcome the mistake:

- Is a plan going to be created (with many constituent groups) that will guide the day-to-day efforts of the parish development efforts?
- Is the plan going to address the six main areas of Catholic Parish Development:
  - » Constituent records,
  - » Fund development,
  - » Communication,
  - » Total stewardship process,
  - » People engagement,
  - » Special events.
- Do you have a core team in place that will help facilitate the process?
- Have you assessed what you are presently doing?

MISTAKE #4: *The people in charge of the parish development effort have very little support and few training opportunities in order to grow and improve.*

Questions to ask to overcome the mistake:

- What services does the diocese offer in regard to monitoring and training?
- Are there reputable workshops in your area and beyond that you can go to and learn more about Catholic Parish Development?
- What kinds of resources are you assembling in your parish development library?
- Do the people working in parish development in your diocese get together (formally or informally) to simply talk about what is working and what is not?

MISTAKE #5: *The development effort is not built around a strong "people fuel" component—one where 50–100 new people are invited every year to get involved in some meaningful manner.*

Questions to ask to overcome the mistake:

- What are we doing to address the first I: *Identify?* Are we constantly adding to a list the names of people who can make a difference?
- Do the leaders understand the importance of "empowering the laity"?
- Are there good and clear processes set up for people to become involved?
- Are all invitations to people made personally?
- Is the pastor the one to issue the invitation?

MISTAKE #6: *When people are invited to form a planning team, or some development committee, the 60%–40% rule is not used. (60% of the people invited are new to involvement; 40% are already involved)*

Questions to ask to overcome the mistake:

- What process is in place to identify the 60% "new" people to your parish—on a regular basis?
- Is prayer used in discerning which people to invite to which group or team?
- Do all development leaders understand the meaning of the 60%–40% rule?
- Do all development leaders understand that this 60–40 rule is key to the success of the development efforts?

MISTAKE #7: *The total stewardship process (one of the six main areas of CPD) is all about money.*

Questions to ask to overcome the mistake:

- When parish leaders talk about "stewardship" do they mainly mean money?

- If you have a "stewardship report" or "corner" in your Sunday bulletin, is it mainly reporting what was collected the previous weekend?
- Do you emphasize the importance of all three areas of total stewardship?
- Is the culture of the parish "money first and then people" or just the opposite?

MISTAKE #8: *Parishes launch into a capital campaign without taking the proper steps to build people support and establish a strong development stance.*

Questions to ask to overcome the mistake:
- Does the parish have a long-range pastoral plan in place for all areas—not just facilities?
- Who made the decision to do what is going to be done?
- Is the campaign going to advance the spiritual life of the parish?
- Does the campaign tie into the mission and vision of the institution?
- Is there confidence in the leadership?
- Has there been excellent communication to all "publics"?
- Has there been successful annual giving?
- Is the infrastructure for parish development in place?

MISTAKE #9: *Parish leaders do not understand the juxtaposition of the fund-raising events to offertory giving to capital giving to endowed giving to planned giving.*

Questions to ask to overcome the mistake:
- Are the parish fund-raisers carefully planned and strategically scheduled so as not to interfere with other development $$$ efforts?
- Is there a strong parish offertory giving effort in place that is equated with the stewardship of finance efforts?
- Is a capital campaign seen as essential every ten years?

- What money is used to "fuel" the endowment efforts?
- Is there an organized planned giving process in place?

MISTAKE #10: *Parish leaders do not understand that the stewardship of finance effort is the single most important development $$$ effort that could ever be done.*
Questions to ask to overcome the mistake:
- Are the dollar goals for the stewardship of finance effort realistic or based solely on budget projections?
- Is there a 10%–15% increase in the number of people who participate from year to year in the total stewardship efforts?
- What is the attrition rate in the stewardship of finance efforts over the past five years?
- Are parish fund-raisers "stepping on the toes" of the stewardship of finance effort year after year?
- Is the stewardship of finance effort evaluated each year by the people who support it?
- Is there an annual report each year of what is done with the money?

MISTAKE #11: *Direct mail, social media, and e-mail are seen as the main tools for inviting people.*
Questions to ask to overcome the mistake:
- Do parish leaders understand that direct mail, social media, and e-mail should be used for three major things: introduce and announce, position, reinforce, but never to "totally convince"?
- Is there an in-person method for inviting people?

MISTAKE #12: *The pastor does not have to get directly involved in the development efforts.*
Questions to ask to overcome the mistake:
- What is the role of the pastor in the development efforts at your parish?

- Does the pastor see development as a nuisance or a necessity?
- Does he build into his schedule a regular meeting time with the development leaders of the parish?
- Will the pastor sit down one-on-one and invite the gifts?
- Has the pastor been educated on what development is and what it is not?

MISTAKE #13: *The parish staff are not seen as being key players in the development process.*
Questions to ask to overcome the mistake:
- Do parish leaders understand that the parish staff are very important to the development effort? They are the ones who live out the mission every day.
- What communication vehicles are in place to invite and involve them?
- Do any of the staff serve as members of the core team or on a planning team?
- Do staff members have the opportunity to ask questions and give input?
- Do the development leaders ask what needs the staff may have?
- If you have a development director, is she/he present for all staff meetings?

MISTAKE #14: *There is no core team to help steer the day-to-day development activities of the parish.*
Questions to ask to overcome the mistake:
- Who is in charge of the development efforts?
- Is this a one-person show, or are there shared responsibilities?
- Does the development director try and do everything by himself/herself?
- Are there 15+ members of a core team?
- Have they been trained?
- Does the core team work side by side with the development director?

- If there is no development director, is there a core team member who is in charge?

MISTAKE #15: *The parish database is not kept up-to-date and does not have the ability to manage the relationships in the parish.*

Questions to ask to overcome the mistake:
- Who is in charge of the database efforts?
- Does the software have the capability to keep track of all gifts?
- Does the software have the capability to keep track of important conversations and notes?
- Does the software have the capability to run accurate reports?
- Does the software work also as a CRM (Customer Relationship Management) tool?

Questions, Exercises, and Next Best Steps for Lesson Fifteen

1. Of the fifteen mistakes listed above, which ones do you believe your parish needs to improve on? Please explain.

2. Of the fifteen mistakes listed above, which ones do you believe you are right on track with and are not weak areas of your parish development efforts? Please explain.

3. After completing Section III of the book, how close do you believe your parish is to launching or continuing a vibrant parish development effort—one which follows many of the concepts and principles of this book? Please explain.

4. In 100 words or less, please summarize what you have learned and discussed in reading this book on Catholic Parish Development.

PART IV

Catholic Parish Development Pyramid of Success

I began writing *Total Parish Development* in January 2018. After working with Catholic parishes since 1989 and realizing that we do not share a common language around development, stewardship, and evangelization, I began by articulating what is meant by these three words in Lesson Two. As I have seen through the years, the word *development* is the hardest of the three to explain—which ultimately became the overall purpose of the book—to not only explain but to illustrate and show the processes of Catholic Parish Development. As Father Jim Manning said earlier in Lesson Two,

> *Development* is the ministry that puts a face on *stewardship*. As a ministry in the church, *development* provides the structures, the processes, and the avenues by which the People of God can do and live the spirituality of *stewardship*. *Development* helps the People of God live *stewardship* in an organized fashion. *Development*, as a ministry, positions the People of God on the same page and heading in the same direction as they live the gospel call to *stewardship*. *Development* helps the People of God live out their baptismal right and responsibility to be involved in the life of the church and thus share in the building of the Kingdom of God here on earth. *Development* helps accompany people in the journey of life back to the Kingdom; it is the conduit for people

engagement and true stewardship. In the process of fulfilling the call to *stewardship* in the ministry of *development, evangelization* is being done. *Evangelization* is preaching the Good News of Jesus.

I knew when I finished the outline of the book that the above three definitions would be crucial for the reader to understand, because if these words are not understood then Catholic Parish Development would be lost and mixed up with the word stewardship, and development and stewardship would be seen as being synonymous. As we all know, stewardship is strong enough to stand on its own two feet; we just need to make sure we know where and how it fits in terms of developing the parish.

Since I was young, I have always lived and loved the game of basketball. Our whole family played, and I have a daughter who is currently playing college basketball at Millsaps in Jackson, Mississippi. In spring 2018, I was trying to find some motivational and educational materials for her to read over the summer. It was then that I revisited John Wooden's famous *Pyramid of Success: Lessons on Leadership*. Back in my basketball coaching days in Catholic schools, this book offered a wonderful model to follow in working with young players. In viewing it again after many years, a light bulb went on! Although quite different in purpose and language, the concept of creating a pyramid of success for Catholic parishes to understand development became a major focus for over four months. And so, after many revisions, and with the help of Ryan Zellner, ISPD's communication guru, we created this pyramid. In actuality, the pyramid is a summary of this entire book on one sheet of paper. We have even taken the image and created posters, and if you have gotten this far in the book, please e-mail me at fedonaldson@ispd.com, and we will send you a free poster suitable for framing or posting in your office.

Let's start at the top and then go to the bottom of the pyramid and then move through the seven tiers. Everything you have learned thus far should come alive in this pyramid.

CATHOLIC PARISH DEVELOPMENT
BRINGING PEOPLE TO CHRIST AND CHRIST TO PEOPLE

"The greatest challenge we face in our Catholic parishes today is to create the roadways, avenues, and vehicles to invite, involve, and engage people."

"A Catholic parish is only going to attract as many resources (people, finances, community, etc.) as it deserves to attract. And what it deserves to attract will always be in direct relationship to the quality of its leadership, vision, uniqueness, and people-engaging culture."

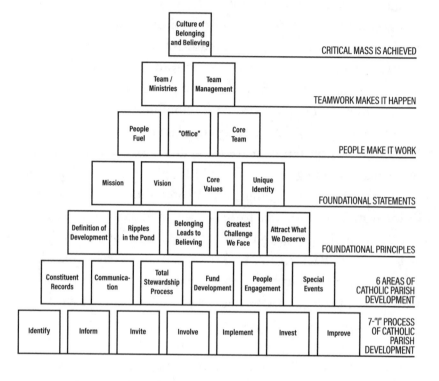

ACTIVE SIGNS OF A BELONGING CULTURE

1. Win-Win Relationships
2. Welcoming/Engaging Processes
3. Collaborative Vision
4. Transparency/Truthfulness
5. Numerous Spiritual Growth Opportunities
6. Consistently Seeking Input
7. Personal Relationship Building
8. "Warm" Church/"Alive" Liturgies
9. Small Faith Communities
10. Continuous Improvement

The title of the pyramid is *Catholic Parish Development: Bringing People to Christ and Christ to People*. That is the ultimate goal of a true parish development effort. All of the processes, all of the planning, all of the "people fuel" activities are all geared to bring people into a closer relationship with Christ. This is why you, as part of the leadership in your Catholic parish, should want to learn, organize, and implement a vibrant parish development effort. We can never lose sight of this goal; it should be the driver and motivator for everything you do in setting up this parish development system.

Recently, I presented the concept of parish development to a group of ministry leaders in a very large parish in the Midwest. I had been invited to talk about how to engage that 70% that is either uninvolved or actively disengaged. After I went through many entry levels of identifying, informing, and inviting, and showing the value of these steps, one parish leader raised her hand and said, "All of this sounds so business-like. Is this really necessary? Do we really need to conduct surveys and form teams and have a strategic plan and identify our vision? After all, we just need to preach the gospel message to people."

I have heard the point she was making numerous times, and it is a valid one. It reminds me of an old friend of mine who was a marine in World War II. He once shared this life lesson: "You know, Frank, before we could move inland and make progress, we had to land on the beach first and secure that position." I have never forgotten what he said, and I often use it as an answer to what this lady said at that large parish. There are so many people who have fallen away from the church, who have fallen away from any form of religion, and who simply do not participate in liturgy except at Christmas, Easter, and when a child needs to be baptized, a daughter needs to be married, or a family member needs to be buried. Because I have spoken to so many of these people through the years, I believe I can say that 90% need a meaningful entry point, and oftentimes that entry point is when someone will personally reach out and invite him/her to something—usually social—where the sense of belonging comes alive. True Catholic Parish Development provides the processes and lights the way—with the ultimate goal of bringing people to Christ and Christ to people.

At the top left of the Parish Pyramid of Success is the quote you have seen before: "The greatest challenge we face in our Catholic parishes today is to create the roadways, avenues, and vehicles to invite, involve, and engage people." So much of what we present in *Total Parish Development* is about showing how to solve that challenge.

At the top right is the other quote—just as important, "A Catholic parish is only going to attract as many resources (people, finances, community, etc.) as it deserves to attract. And what it deserves to attract will always be in direct relationship to the quality of its leadership, vision, uniqueness, and people-engaging culture." I believe this statement says it all.

At the bottom of the Parish Pyramid of Success, you will see the 10 Active Signs of a Belonging Culture. These are the themes and principles that run through the fifteen lessons of the book.

- Win-Win Relationships
- Welcoming/Engaging Processes
- Collaborative Vision
- Transparency/Truthfulness
- Numerous Spiritual Growth Opportunities
- Consistently Seeking Input
- Personal Relationship Building
- "Warm" Church/"Alive" Liturgies
- Small Faith Communities
- Continuous Improvement

There are seven tiers on the pyramid, all of which provide an outline for what has been covered in *Total Parish Development*. Let's begin at the base of the pyramid:

TIER VII: 7-"I" PROCESS OF CATHOLIC PARISH DEVELOPMENT

- Identify
- Inform

- Invite
- Involve
- Implement
- Invest
- Improve

As we have stated throughout, the 7-"I" process provides the "base line" for parish development to flourish. Lesson One discusses each of these elements, what they mean, and why they need to be seen in a systemic way.

TIER VI: **6** AREAS OF CATHOLIC PARISH DEVELOPMENT

- Constituent Records
- Communication
- Total Stewardship Process
- Fund Development
- People Engagement
- Special Events

In order for parish development to be understood and organized, we believe that these six organizational areas need to be the focus points. Lesson Six is devoted to showing these areas in an organizational chart and explaining the meaning of each.

TIER V: FOUNDATIONAL PRINCIPLES

- Definition of Development
- Ripples in the Pond
- Belonging Leads to Believing
- Greatest Challenge We Face
- Attract What We Deserve

All of these principles are shown in the book. The first three bullet points are all in Lesson One, and the last two bullet points are at the top right and top left of the pyramid.

TIER IV: FOUNDATIONAL STATEMENTS

- Mission

- Vision
- Core Values
- Unique Identity

These are the statements that all parish leaders should be able to articulate—both in the spoken and in the written word. Lesson Ten shows the value of having these foundational statements.

TIER III: PEOPLE MAKE IT WORK
- People Fuel
- "Office"
- Core Team

These three bullet points are key points on the organizational chart for Catholic Parish Development in Lesson Six.

TIER II: TEAMWORK MAKES IT HAPPEN
- Teams/Ministries
- Team Management

The ability of a parish to build teams and to have a teamwork mentality in all ministries will mean the difference between a vibrant parish and a parish that operates in carefully designed boxes.

TIER I: CRITICAL MASS IS ACHIEVED

A very important or crucial stage of Catholic Parish Development—where activity acquires self-sustaining viability—is when a parish reaches "critical mass." It is believed that the parish can then remain viable and prevail and not just survive. Another way of looking at "critical mass" is to know the number of people who become fully engaged in the life of the parish where they not only promote what is going on but become the symbols of a belonging and believing culture.

It is our belief that through these seven tiers, two quotes, and ten active signs on the Parish Development Pyramid of Success we will be able to bring people to Christ and Christ to people.

PART V

Closing Thoughts

> It is Jesus who stirs in you the desire to do something great with your lives, the will to follow an ideal, the refusal to allow yourselves to be ground down by mediocrity, the courage to commit yourselves humbly and patiently to improving yourselves and society, making the world more human and more fraternal.
>
> SAINT JOHN PAUL II

Throughout this book and throughout my work with parishes throughout the country, I have tried to motivate parish leaders to go *to total parish development*. Sometimes this has been easy to do because the leadership "got it," and other times all I heard was, "We've always done things this way. Why change?" There are two main reasons why I believe so strongly in Catholic Parish Development. 1) I have seen it be successful time after time. 2) Today we live in a totally different time and era where the challenges we face now are scary. We must develop; we must move beyond. Just view these quotes.

"From 2014 to 2017, an average of 39% of Catholics reported attending church in the past seven days. This is down from an average of 45% from 2005 to 2008 and represents a steep decline from 75% in 1955" (Gallup, April 9, 2018).

"There were approximately 46 million Catholics in the United States in 1965, and 55% of them were attending Sunday Mass on a weekly basis. Today, we have a whopping 73 million Catholics in our country, but only 23% attend Mass on a weekly basis. This equates to 8 million fewer Catholics at Mass each Sunday than were there in 1965" (CARA, 2018).

The facts and figures presented above are coming from two reliable sources: CARA (The Center for Applied Research in the Apostolate) and Gallup, Inc.

Living in south Louisiana all my life, I equate this to the erosion of the Louisiana coastline, which has been called to everyone's attention over the past twenty-five years, with many news outlets screaming the following headlines on a regular basis: "Louisiana's coastline is disappearing at the rate of a football field an hour" (NOLA.com 2017). Although there are a handful of people who are on top of this and seeking to come up with the funding and the resources to stop the bleeding, many people shake their head and say, "What a shame. *They* better do something about that" (that great mysterious *they*).

After all these years of consults, workshops, online classes, and visits, if there is one thing I know to be true it is this: *The solutions, processes, and plans that a Catholic parish used to get them to where they are today should not be the same solutions that will get that parish to where they need to go in the future.*

Each and every parish must reinvent itself in some way every 5–10 years. Now I know you have heard that before, but I believe what I am saying is different, and this is a theme we have been promoting for years. Let me restate it: *Each and every individual Catholic parish must reinvent itself every 5–10 years.* The difference is the ownership and the responsibility rests with that individual parish. The pastor, the parish council, the parish staff—the spark should begin here, and then parishioners and other stakeholders need to make it happen.

The obvious question is: Make what happen? And the answer is: make parish development happen so you can address and move forward with the following:

- How you welcome new parishioners;
- How you invite people to belong;
- How you seek input from all parish families;
- How you personally relate and meet with each parish family;

- How you become an "amazing parish" by offering professional growth opportunities to all parishioners;
- How you communicate with all parish families;
- How you collaborate with your parochial school (if applicable);
- How you engage Hispanic families in your parish;
- How you become a total stewardship parish;
- How you evangelize;
- How your parish becomes a stronger beacon of hope for the community in which you reside;
- How you partner with neighboring parishes—Catholic and Protestant;
- How you further involve and engage lay leadership of the parish;
- How you help your parishioners discover what talents and gifts they would want to share with the parish;
- How you help all of your parish families afford to send their children to a Catholic school;
- How you better plan for the future;
- How you share this dynamic new vision;
- How you communicate to all families that this parish is theirs;
- How you set up a vibrant parish development effort to succeed.

We would never have entertained many of these thoughts fifty years ago. This is a new era and our models from yesterday have drastically changed: believing does not lead to belonging, faith in church leaders has eroded, demographics have shifted, competition has increased, and technology has certainly changed the game. We are living in a time where, if we are not at the top of our game, our chances of survival are lessened. We must not take the position of, "Oh well" or "The diocese will take care of us." No! Each and every diocese has their own set of challenges. We—each individual parish—must step forward, throw away old habits from the past, pour new wine into new wineskins, and really flourish—not just survive. This begins with you and me. Catholic Parish Development is a viable answer if you want to move *to total parish development*.

AFTERWORD

The Founding of the Institute for School and Parish Development

In the 1950s, I was raised in the Episcopal church in Slidell, Louisiana, and from the time I was in elementary school through high school and on through my college years, the Episcopal church was where I practiced my faith. My mom was very active in the Ladies Altar Society, and my dad was a member of the Board of Vestry. My brother Don and I were acolytes, and when the minister was on vacation, Don and I did the readings at the "Sunday Morning Prayer Service" for the congregation of 100+ families. Christ Church Episcopal in Slidell, Louisiana, was one of the anchors of family activity—Bible study, covered dish suppers, monthly parish picnics, home visits from the pastor, recreational activities, and other opportunities for fellowship. (In fact, the first real "date" I ever had was with a high school girl who sang in the youth choir.) Most of the families did not view Christ Church Episcopal as just a place to visit once a week; parish families and individuals joined together in a wide range of activities and events. We all felt part of a family.

Time marched on, and I was introduced to the Catholic faith when I attended De La Salle High School in New Orleans. The La Sallian Christian Brothers had a positive and profound impact on my life, and there were several Brothers who were responsible for me getting involved in the teaching profession. At De La Salle, I became exposed to the Mass, participated in religion classes, developed wonderful relationships with many of the Christian Brothers, and came to realize that there was a richness in the Catholic faith that was inspiring and refreshing. I also realized that the Catholic faith and the Episcopal faith had many commonalities, which led me to further discovery of Roman Catholicism.

I graduated from college with a teaching degree in English and went on to gain advanced degrees while teaching in Catholic schools in New Orleans and Lafayette, Louisiana. Prompted by my involvement in Catholic schools, in 1974, at the age of 30, and under the guidance of Father Paul Lamberty, I embraced the Roman Catholic faith at Immaculate Conception Church in Marrero, Louisiana. This allowed me to grow further in my faith; however, as the years passed on, I came to realize that something was missing—something that was present at Christ Church Episcopal but was not present in the Catholic parishes where we worshiped.

In 1986, I took a position as an English teacher at Mercy Academy in New Orleans, Louisiana. After my first year of teaching sophomore English, the principal asked me if I would be interested in also becoming the development director. She explained that the school needed to do more than hold a candy drive and send out pledge cards to alumnae asking them for money. We needed to communicate better; we needed to write grants; we needed to create a monthly newsletter—all those things that many Catholic schools did when they first got into development back in the 1980s and early '90s. Having written grants and having put together a song and dance group of 100 young people to perform 150 shows at the 1984 New Orleans World's Fair, where we had to raise over $500,000 on our own, I knew that I had basic skills in promotion and marketing. My English major had helped me become a decent writer, and performing all the time gave me the experience to be in front of people and lead a team or make a presentation.

After one year, I came to the realization that development worked when people became involved in the process. *Belonging leads to believing.* We built teams to share their best wisdom in planning for the future of the school; we built teams for the annual appeal; we built alumnae teams to invite and bring back more alums on campus; we reached out to the 30+ parishes who were the feeder sources for our students; we brought past parents back to campus; we started business lunches and involved our students in the alumnae phonathon. In essence, we built up our faith community by engaging people and not just asking them for money. We were successful in bringing people together. In 18 months, we personally identified, invited, and involved over 250 new people/ families in the life of the school. Our student enrollment increased by 25%; our volunteer involvement level increased by 30%; more than 200 new alumnae came back to campus for fun activities; our special events were packed with new faces and new energy; and, the participation in our Annual Appeal increased by 25%.

In my third year in development, I had three local parishes contact me to see if I was interested in consulting with them. And so, in 1989, ISPD (Institute for School and Parish Development) was born with the mission statement: *Bringing people, process, and ministry together to help build the Kingdom of God.* Our work with Catholic schools, parishes, and dioceses had begun.

Since 1989, we have worked with hundreds of Catholic institutions from coast to coast—from All Hallows Parish in LaJolla, California, to Our Lady of Lourdes in Slidell, Louisiana, to National Shrine of the Little Flower Basilica in Royal Oak, Michigan, to St. Mary of the Assumption Parish in Springboro, Ohio, to all of the Catholic schools in the five dioceses in New Jersey, to St. Jude Cathedral in St. Petersburg, Florida, to St. Thomas Aquinas Catholic Church in Alpharetta, Georgia, to the Archdiocese of Baltimore, where we spent three days working with all priests in the archdiocese on how to engage more people into the life of their parishes. Over 2,000,000 miles on Delta and over 100 nights per year in Marriott Courtyards. It has been quite a journey—and it continues.